IN THE MESQUITE

by

STEVE HODEL

STEVE HODEL

IN THE MESQUITE

The Solving of the 1938
West Texas Kidnap Torture Murders
of Hazel and Nancy Frome

by

STEVE HODEL

ISBN-13: 9780996045728

Printed in the United States of America 1098765432

Cover design: Robert J. Sadler

THOUGHTPRINT PRESS
LOS ANGELES, CALIFORNIA

Dedication

For the victims, living and dead.

ALSO, BY STEVE HODEL

~

Black Dahlia Avenger
(Arcade/Skyhorse 2015)

Most Evil
(Dutton 2009)

Black Dahlia Avenger II
(Thoughtprint Press 2014)

Most Evil II
(Rare Bird Books 2015)

Black Dahlia Avenger III
(Rare Bird Books 2018)

"It [*Frome investigation*] remains the biggest unsolved mystery in the American Southwest."

Texas Rangers, Department of Public Safety

AND NOW COMES

IN THE MESQUITE

The Solving of the 1938 West Texas Kidnap Torture Murders of Hazel and Nancy Frome

Today, some eighty-one years after the double-homicide occurred, the names of Hazel and Nancy Frome are long forgotten. The cold case now no more significant than a couple of dried out tumbleweeds that have come to rest on a lonely stretch of highway in the desert sand near Phantom Lake, a few miles from the small West Texas town of Van Horn.

However, in April 1938, the names of Hazel and Nancy Frome were *big news* and could be found headlined, above the fold, on nearly every newspaper in the nation.

The breaking story began slowly, announcing that a mother and daughter, traveling in their touring car, cross-country from California to the East Coast, "were missing on a Texas highway."

Within days came a second announcement cautioning that "foul play was suspected." Next, their abandoned car was found, and on the fifth day of the search, the nation's worst fears were realized.

In just five days, we see hope turn to horror and become what some of the press dubbed, *The Mesquite Murders,* which, seven decades later, remains—Texas' greatest unsolved murder mystery.

Below, we follow the original headline reportage as it literally unfolded, day-by-day:

Sunday – April 3, 1938

2 WOMEN TOURISTS VANISH IN TEXAS

Sunday – April 3, 1938

Wichita Daily Times 31,000

TWO MISSING WOMEN BELIEVED SLAIN

CAR FOUND ON HIGHWAY NEAR PECOS

Monday – April 4, 1938

Corsicana Daily Sun

SEEK BRUTAL KILLER 2 WOMEN

Friday – April 8, 1938

The Victims

In March of 1938, Mrs. Hazel Frome, age 50, and her eldest daughter, Nancy, age 23, decided to take a cross-country trip from their home in Berkeley, California. Their purpose, to visit Nancy's younger sister, Mada, recently married and living with her soldier-husband, Lt. Benjamin McMakin, at the Parris Island Marine Corp base in South Carolina.

The father and family patriarch, Weston Frome, also age 50, was a prominent Berkeley businessman and had recently won a brand-new touring car [a 1937 Packard Series-Eight, 7-seater] in a twenty-five-cent raffle. "Pop" Weston gifted the new car to his daughter Nancy, as her graduation present from U.C. Berkeley. Mother and daughter would road test the machine by making the trip east. They planned to be gone for two months and anticipated the cross-country trip would take just six days.

OAKLAND TRIBUNE. MONDAY, APRIL 4, 1938

HOME OF BERKELEY KIDNAP-MURDER VICTIMS

Frome Home

Nancy Frome Posing

This is the Berkeley home at 2560 Cedar Street which Mrs. Hazel Frome and her daughter, Nancy, left 12 days ago for a vacation trip East. Also shown is a new picture of ...

What follows is a detailed reconstruction of Hazel and Nancy's travel timeline, and known movements, as provided by law enforcement, family, and friends, and reliable citizen-witnesses who had direct contact with the two women in the week, days, and hours, immediately before their abduction. While many of the eye-witness interviews were not received by law enforcement for days or weeks following the murders,

I am presenting them here as a chronological reconstruction as the sightings actually occurred in real time.

Wednesday, March 23, 1938- 12 noon

Hazel and Nancy Frome have their gray Packard loaded with expensive luggage and depart from their home in Berkeley, California and drive south to Los Angeles, where they checked in for an overnight stay at the luxurious 1500 room Biltmore Hotel. The Biltmore was considered then, as now, to be one of the finest hotels on the West Coast.

[Trivia Note- The Biltmore Hotel, less than a decade later, would play an important role in what would become L.A.'s most infamous murder. The hotel was reportedly the last known location, the victim, Elizabeth "Black Dahlia" Short was seen leaving before her abduction and murder. (The Black Dahlia's "Missing Week" would later be proven to be a myth with a dozen reported sightings of the victim by witnesses six of whom knew her personally and could not have been mistaken.) As fate would have it, Mrs. Hazel Frome and Elizabeth Short also shared the same birthdate—July 29th.]

BILTMORE HOTEL, Los Angeles California

Thursday, March 24, 1938

Hazel and Nancy departed Los Angeles in their brand-new Packard touring car and drove to Phoenix, AZ where they stayed overnight at the Sea Breeze Motel.

Friday, March 25, 1938

Late afternoon, mother and daughter arrived in downtown El Paso, Texas and checked into another five-star hotel—The Cortez.

Registered and given suite 814 at The Cortez, Mrs. Frome immediately contacted the concierge and advised him that they were having "car trouble, the engine was sputtering" and needed to have their new Packard checked out. The car was driven by hotel staff to a local repair shop to be examined.

HOTEL CORTEZ, El Paso, Texas

Saturday, March 26, 1938

The Packard dealership mechanic informed the Fromes "the repairs would take at least three days as they had to send away for parts."

Stuck in town, the two women decided to make the best of it and went to Juarez, Mexico, which was just a short twenty-minute trolley ride from their luxury hotel. Both women were seen later that afternoon, in the hotel lobby, carrying shopping bags filled with their purchases from across the border.

International Trolley El Paso to Juarez, Mexico

Sunday, March 27, 1938

Hazel and Nancy contacted a Mr. Harold White, a local El Paso resident, an employee of their father's company who invited them to join his family for the day. The Fromes were given a tour of El Paso and again went to Juarez where they enjoyed some fine dining with the White family.

Monday, March 28, 1938

Hazel and Nancy again traveled across the border and had dinner at the *Café Juarez*.

Witness Keno Smith, the floor manager, would later inform detectives that he observed: "two smartly dressed Americans males, both in business suits approach the Fromes and ask them to dance." On that occasion, he believed the women declined, and the two men left the café. Smith also let slip to detectives that he thought he had recognized one of the men as being in the café on prior occasions, but then caught himself and became evasive indicating he could be mistaken.

A second witness, Mr. B.N. Gist, and his unidentified male friend were also in the *Café Juarez* seated close by the Fromes at a table just a few feet away.

Gist watched as the two males approached the women with their hats in hands and overheard Mrs. Frome tell one of the men that she was "sure she had seen or met him before on the Pacific Coast."

Gist then heard the two men invite the Fromes to

"join their party across the street at the *Tivoli Café.*" He informed detectives that both men were polite and well-dressed, and he was unsure if the Fromes accepted their invitation but recalled seeing the two men leave the *Café Juarez,* while the Fromes stayed and finished their drinks.

Hazel and Nancy Frome invited by two males to "join their party at the Tivoli Café for dancing." (Not known if they accepted?)

Both women returned to the Cortez Hotel at approximately 11:00 p.m. and obtained their room key from the night clerk.

Tuesday, March 29, 1938

Mid-morning, Hazel walked to a nearby beauty salon for a pre-scheduled hair appointment. The owner of the beauty shop, Mr. E.L. Bradfort, would later inform detectives that while Mrs. Frome was having her hair done, he observed a man standing outside the salon staring in and watching her through the window. Bradfort described the man as: "Male 35-38, medium-slender build, business suit wearing a dress hat." The man remained outside, and when Mrs. Frome exited the business the man approached her, they had a short conversation, and then the two walked down the street together. Mr. Bradfort was later shown various photographs of individuals fitting the description but never made any identification of this unknown male.

Mr. Toby Martin, the owner of the *Martin Travel Bureau*, located nearby the Cortez Hotel, provided another curious conversation with the Fromes on Tuesday, the day before their departure.

Both women entered his travel agency and informed him they were "looking for a companion to accompany them on the ride from El Paso to Dallas" adding, "a presentable man would do, and there would be no charge to him for the trip." Martin informed them that he knew of no one that might want to make the trip at such short notice. The women left the business, and there was no further contact.

Late afternoon both women again took the trolley to Juarez and dined at the *Spanish Town Café,* then went to a nearby nightclub for after dinner drinks.

Club employees would later inform police that both women were seen dancing with two men. Upon returning to the Cortez and obtaining their key, the clerk gave Hazel **a wrapped package which simply bore the hand-printed name "FROME."** No information was discovered on who had left the package. A hotel employee recalled that Mrs. Frome appeared a little tipsy, and it was his impression she had been drinking.

Wednesday, March 30, 1938

Cortez Hotel maid, Maria Baca, was interviewed and reported seeing both women in Suite 814 on the morning of their departure. Miss Baca spoke little English but informed detectives that she observed both mother and daughter reading from a letter on the desk. While she could not understand what was being said, she noted that both became visibly upset, fearful, and it was the maid's impression that the contents of the letter had caused them to want to hurriedly pack and leave the hotel. [SKH Note- Based on Miss Baca's statements and observation, the contents of this letter became of primary interest to investigators; however, the letter was never located.]

The Fromes checked out of the Cortez Hotel at 11:30 a.m. and stopped to have their repaired Packard gassed at a nearby Texaco service station. The attendant, when later interviewed by the police, informed authorities that the two women "seemed very nervous and in a hurry and declined his offer to check the Packard's oil and tire pressure." The attendant told detectives they left his station at 12:10 p.m.

Several important eye-witnesses came forward and provided valuable information on having seen the two women, and their distinctive Packard, and provided separate, but consistent descriptions of their possible kidnappers.

Witness Chauncey Worchester, of Newburyport, Massachusetts, after reading about the horrific murders in the newspaper, wrote two separate letters to authorities describing seeing both women on the road on Wednesday, March 30th. He was contacted and interviewed by the FBI at his home and provided the following information Mr. Worchester was traveling on Route 80 with his parents and a friend and made two separate sightings of the Frome women and their 1937 Packard.

The first was when his car passed theirs on Wednesday, early afternoon. The Frome Packard was stopped at the side of the highway. He observed an older woman seated inside in the front passenger seat and a younger woman standing outside with her foot on the vehicle's running board. A black sedan was parked nearby, and he believes two individuals were standing between the two parked cars. A third male was seen getting out of the sedan.

Several hours later, and approximately fifty miles from the first sighting the Worchesters observed the same two cars traveling at a high rate of speed. The Packard was being driven by the younger woman with the older still seated next to her with a possible passenger in the rear seat. The black sedan, which he described as a "possible Ford or Chevy" was following close behind the Packard. Chancey informed the FBI agents that it was his impression that, "the driver [Nancy Frome] appeared to be driving against her will and very nervous."

As the Worchesters were following behind the Packard and black sedan which were far ahead on U.S.

80 were seen to make a right turn at the San Antonio Junction. The Worchesters made a left and took the Dallas route.

Without question, the single most important eye-witness in the Frome investigation was a trucker who made regular deliveries along Highway 80. His name was Jim Milam. This witness made three separate sightings of the victims and their probable abductors, all in the afternoon hours of Wednesday, March 30, 1938.

Milam was making his regular deliveries along Highway 80 and was driving his truck east in Hudspeth County, some six miles west of Sierra Blanca, Texas, which is 107 miles east of El Paso.

At about 1:30 p.m. Milam observed the Frome Packard pass him heading east on Highway 80. It was

Highway 80 near Sierra Blanca, Texas

being chased by a second car which **he described** as, **"A black coach or sedan**. He described the car as having **"white letters within a white border on the passenger door**."

Milam saw a male driving the black sedan and **"a woman with blonde or red hair** was sitting next to him. It looked like she was straddling the gearshift. She was **wearing a bonnet** like they type you see a Salvation Army woman wear. It was tied under her chin."

Milam went on to say, "the black sedan had two separate license plates. One appeared to be a Texas plate that was flapping in the wind." The second license plate he didn't recognize. He continued to follow the cars through Sierra Blanca but then lost sight of the vehicle.

At approximately 3:00 p.m. that same day **Milam** was continuing on his delivery route, and when he was six miles west of Van Horn, Texas, he again came across the same dark colored vehicle. However, **this time**, it was being **driven by** the **woman with the bonnet. He again noted the distinctive white lettering on the driver's doo**r, but acknowledged to authorities that he "was illiterate, *and could not read the writing written on the door panel.*"

[SKH Note-How ironic. Had this witness been able to read the words printed on the suspect vehicle' door, this case could very likely have been solved within a week of its occurrence.]

At this juncture, he noted a third car, driven by a second woman, pull off the highway, near the Wild Horse Creek Bridge. He observed a man walk towards this third car and Milam pulled to the side of the road and watched as the male got in this car and it drove west, passing him and heading back toward Van Horn, Texas. Milam continued east on Highway 80 delivering his product to his customers.

Late in the afternoon on Wednesday, Milam observed the Frome Packard pass him one final time. It was driven at high speed, by a lone male, followed closely by the dark sedan, driven by the woman still wearing the bonnet.

Milam did not come forward as a witness to report what he had seen to the local sheriff until Friday, April 1, after hearing about the discovery of the abandoned Packard and the two "missing women." His story would not be made public until after the finding of the bodies on Sunday, April 3, 1938.

Thursday, March 31, 1938

A group of Army engineer surveyors reports the Frome Packard abandoned near Phantom Lake, some 11 miles west of the small Texas town of Balmorhea, near the intersection of Highways 80 and 290. The engineers called the local sheriff and reported initially seeing the car parked at the location, the previous afternoon.

Deputy Sam Davis of the Reeves County Sheriff's Office responded to the call and found the car doors unlocked, keys in the ignition, and no luggage inside the car. Also, of interest was the fact that one of the car's tires had been changed, but the original bumper jack was not used, indicating some other person than the Fromes likely changed the tire. Deputy Davis drove the car to the town of Balmorhea. A check of the vehicle's California license plate showed the car to be registered to the Fromes in Berkeley, California. In the initial days following the finding of the car the case was handled simply as a "Missing Persons" investigation.

Friday, April 1, 1938

Jim Milam comes forward and reports his observations and the suspicious activities that occurred between the Frome women and the "mysterious black sedan" two days earlier. Clearly, this was the match that lit the fuse, igniting local law enforcement into action and transformed the Frome case from just another "missing" to foul play suspected and a "feared kidnapped" status.

Saturday, April 2, 1938

A large posse was formed and dozens of deputies, aided by local citizens from surrounding counties united in their attempt to locate the two missing women.

Based on witness Milam's observations, the search for the missing women focused on the lonely stretch of Highway 80 from the east side of Van Horn city limits to where the Frome Packard was found nearly sixty miles to the east, near Balmorhea, Texas.

Half the search team worked their way west from the abandoned vehicle while the other half came east from Van Horn.

Sunday, April 3, 1938

On Sunday, April 3, truck driver Milam directed authorities to the approximate area near Wild Horse Creek Bridge, where on the previous Wednesday afternoon he had seen the male suspect walk to and enter the third vehicle driven by a female who then drove west back towards Van Horn, Texas.

A search of this area resulted in Milam and authorities locating tire tracks adjacent to a caliche pit, just south of the highway. The searchers followed these tracks a half-mile into the desert which led them directly to the crime scene and the bodies of Mrs. Hazel Frome and her daughter, Nancy.

The Crime Scene April 3, 1938, 6:00 pm

This is the spot in the sun-baked West Texas brush country where the bodies of Mrs. Hazel Frome and Nancy Frome were found, carefully placed face down by the slayer. Texas State police are shown hunting for clues. They found considerable evidence.

—A. P. Wirephoto.

Witness Jim Milam (in overalls) at crime-scene with deputies

A cursory examination of the two victims by deputies, at the crime-scene, revealed the following:

1. Both bodies were carefully posed and laid out in prone positions, side-by-side.
2. Both women's clothing had been removed, and Nancy was wearing only her panties, shoes, and socks. Her mother, Hazel, was wearing only a slip, girdle, hose, and shoes.
3. Both victims had been beaten severely and had massive blunt force trauma to their heads and faces.

(Deputies indicated the weapon might have been a hammer or a tire-iron.)

4. Robbery, not a motive as valuable diamond jewelry and watch were on the victim's persons.

5. Evidence suggested that Hazel Frome had been dragged from a vehicle to the shallow pit where she lay.

6. Initial observations by authorities indicated that "Nancy Frome had been ravaged" (raped). However, later reports suggested she may not have been sexually assaulted.

7. Nancy Frome was holding a patch of short black hair in her right hand believed to have been torn from her assailant's head during a struggle. She was also *holding a man's bloody handkerchief in her right hand.* A pack of matches was clutched in her left hand.

8. Crime scene drawing. (see next page)

A follow-up search of the immediate and surrounding area of the crime-scene resulted in deputies finding additional evidence. This included: bloody tissues, an empty wine bottle, and most significantly, *"a thin pair of rubber gloves like the type used by physicians"* which had been wrapped in a page from a California newspaper, found at the crime scene.

Additional tire tracks led north from where the bodies lay and led back to Highway 80, where they then pointed to the east to the direction of Balmorhea, where the Frome Packard was abandoned, some 56 miles east of the murder location.

The victims bodies were transported to El Paso, where their autopsies would be conducted.

Original crime scene drawing, and surrounding area prepared by
Texas Department of Public Safety and released to the press and
public by El Paso Sheriff Chris Fox.

Forensic sketch of the crime scene and map of locations where eyewitnesses
reported unusual incidents on US 80, drawn by a DPS criminal investigator.
El Paso Times Collection, di_08907. The Dolph Briscoe Center for
American History, The University of Texas at Austin

See back cover of *In The Mesquite* for a more detailed
reproduction of the map inset above.

Witness, Jim Milam featured on the front page of the
***El Paso Herald-Post*, Monday, April 4, 19**

Crime scene, Frome Packard, Witness Jim Milam.
Weston & Mada Frome (Nancy's younger sister)

Circa Aug 2015 View of Horizon Compared with Horizon in 1970 'Joaquin' Photo

Joaquin at the Frome crime scene, thirty-two years later, 1970.

52

April 2019 Screen Shot of Google Aug 2015 Street View of Horizon on I-10 (looking west toward Van Horn)

See Next Page - - - >

**April 2019 revisit to crime scene
showing approximate position where
Hazel and Nancy Frome's bodies were
posed
by killers.**

[graphic by Robert J. Sadler]

The Autopsies

The autopsies on Hazel and Nancy Frome were conducted by Dr. L.P. Walter, an El Paso Public Health official, and Dr. Willis Waite, the El Paso County Medical Examiner.

Once the victims' bodies were washed clean, the evidence revealed that both women had suffered horrific torture causing the attending physicians to state, "These are the two most heinous murders ever seen in our careers."

Examination of **Nancy Frome's body revealed** the following:

1. Cause of death, "**Gunshot Wound** to head fired at close range."
2. The weapon used was a **.32 caliber**, and the bullet recovered from the head showed it was "steel-jacket and in good condition."
3. Ligature **strangulation** was **apparent**.
4. The victim's body had been **stomped on** so severely that the trauma **ruptured** both her **diaphragm** and *stomach*.
5. **Eight separate burn** scabs were observed to the back of the victim's right hand "one over **each knuckle** of the fingers. These wounds were **inflicted** by her killer **premortem**, by using either **a cigarette or cigar**.

Examination of Mrs. **Hazel Frome's body revealed** the following:

1. Cause of death, "**Gunshot wound** to head." The bullet entered the left temporal region, "level and slightly anterior to the ear."
2. The bullet was badly deformed and was slightly heavier in weight than the slug that killed Nancy and believed to have been fired from a **.38 caliber**, indicating two separate weapons used.
3. **Bite mark** on her left forearm, and a **large piece of flesh** was **missing from the arm**.
4. **Trauma to head and face** and a **broken jaw**.
5. *Face severely swollen and was almost black and her eyes, nose, and mouth were filled with maggots.*
6. **Corset shoulder straps** were **broken**.

The **coroner's estimate** of the **time of death** for both women set at **approximately "2 ½ to 3 days,"** which led to speculation that the victims could have been held captive and tortured elsewhere as it was a full four days from the time they were last seen alive until the bodies were discovered.

[**SKH Note**- While this could be possible, it should be noted that **determining "time of death"** is one of the most **difficult** forensics **to establish, with accuracy**, even more so given the science and technology available in 1938.]

The Evidence

The following listed evidence was sent to the Texas Crime Lab in Austin and booked under El Paso Sheriff's Case No. 9628:

1. A patch of short black hair found in Nancy Frome's right hand.
2. Man's bloody handkerchief.
3. Book of matches found in Nancy Frome's right hand.
4. Crumpled package of "Lucky Strike" cigarettes.
5. Several smoked cigarette butts found near the bodies.
6. Woman's undergarments, shoes, and socks worn by both victims.
7. .32 and possible .38 spent slugs removed from victim's heads.
8. Wine bottle found near the scene.
9. Bloody tissues found near the scene.
10. Old newspapers from San Francisco and Los Angeles found near the scene.
11. One pair of rubber medical gloves found near the crime scene.

In early April, immediately following the recovery of the two bodies and disclosure to the public of most of the horrific details of the torture-murders, the Frome murder investigation became a major newsprint story across the nation. It was front-page news in almost every newspaper in the country.

Due to this national headline coverage, suddenly the jurisdiction and control of the Frome investigation exploded from local county to state and federal. Now, the sheriff's departments from; Balmorhea, Pecos, Van Horn, and El Paso along with the Department of Public Safety (Texas Rangers) in Austin and the F.B.I. were in the hunt. Egos and territorial disputes as turf-wars began to occur, even before the victim's bodies were buried. Texas governor, James Allred immediately assigned half of his entire Texas Ranger manpower to work the case in hopes of bringing it to a quick solution.

Initially, veteran El Paso sheriff, Chris Fox was put in charge as overall "coordinator" and would be the lead investigator out of his office in El Paso.

A $10,000 reward (an exceptionally large amount in 1938 Depression dollars) was offered, which attracted, even more, investigators to the area. (Private investigators, retired cops, and wannabe armchair detectives, all hoping to solve the case for fame and fortune.)

Follow-Up Witnesses

Deputies were inundated with "tips" from citizens most of which led nowhere or were from cranks. However, a few turned out to be legitimate and provided additional leads. Here are several that added to the investigation:

Witness Everett Harmon was a Greyhound Bus driver who contacted Sheriff Chris Fox and provided him with the following information:

On the afternoon hours of Wednesday, March 30, 1938, he was driving his bus on Highway 80 near

Sierra Blanca, Texas and recalled seeing a "dark coach following close behind a silver-colored Packard." The Packard was driven by an older woman, with a younger female seated next to her. Two men were in the dark vehicle which Harmon believed was "either a Ford, Chevy, or Plymouth." The witness recalled the suspect vehicle had two sets of license plates; one he believed was a Texas plate and the second one he was certain was, "*a New Mexico license plate.*"

Another witness, who contacted Sheriff Fox in the days following the murders, was El Paso resident Mrs. Frances Hammer. Traveling with her husband, she reported seeing the two Frome women on Wednesday afternoon, on the highway near Sierra Blanca, Texas. They were seen standing on the road, next to the side of their light-colored Packard. She suggested to her husband that they stop and render assistance, but he replied, "No need. That black car has stopped to help them out." As they slowly drove by, Mrs. Hammer observed a blonde female seated inside the smaller car and got a close look at the man that was with her, whom she described as:

"Male with a sharp chin, prominent nose, and wearing a light-colored fedora hat, a dark coat, and a tan shirt. He had piercing dark eyes and looked like a dope fiend. I know about dope. I'm a nurse."

Mrs. Hammer and her husband continued driving down the highway without stopping, leaving the unknown male and female to assist the stranded Fromes.

As a side-note, Mrs. Hammer reported to the investigators that she had seen the same car and suspects a few days prior on a lonely stretch of highway. **Mrs. Hammer** claimed the car had followed her, then passed in front of her, slowed down and dropped behind her and then passed her again. She **noted that "the car had markings on the door looked like a California Highway Patrol car shield."**

The bodies of Hazel and Nancy Frome were returned to California and the burial services occurred on April 7, *1938, at the Wilson & Keatzer Funeral Chapel* and transferred to the *Sunset View Cemetery,* in Richmond, California for entombment.

[SKH Note- Ironically, this mortuary is just a few miles north of the *Mountain View Cemetery* in Berkeley, where the body of 1947 murder victim, Elizabeth "Black Dahlia" Short was laid to rest. Both cemeteries are in a direct line of sight, across the Bay from the 1990s residence of Dr. George Hill Hodel, Short's killer, who could see both gravesite locations from his 39th-floor penthouse.] See map next page:

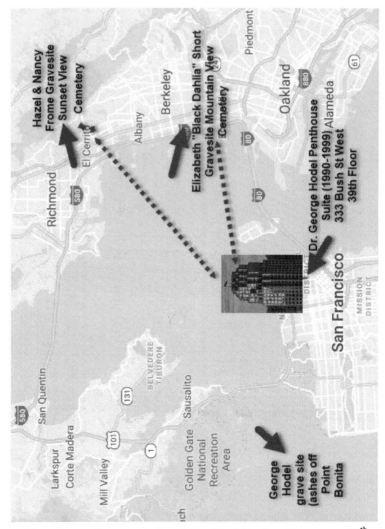

Map shows the proximity of Dr. Hodel's San Francisco 39th floor penthouse residence [1990-1999] to the three murder victims' gravesites.

(top - Sunset View Cemetery – Fromes);

(middle – Mountain View Cemetery – Elizabeth Short)

SUSPECTS

As portrayed in the proverbial 1942 film classic, *Casa Blanca* the word went out from *Sierra Blanca* and the surrounding Texas counties to "round up the usual suspects."

Many of the locally known sex and drug offenders were brought in for questioning and squeezed for information, but nothing stuck.

Initially, the most promising suspect arrested was a Dr. Romano Trotsky. (May 1938 press photo below)

On the back of this original press photograph of Trotsky was printed:

IN CUSTODY May 7, 1938

San Angelo, Tex Dr. Romano Nicholas Trotsky who is being held here in connection with the Frome murder investigation. He claims to be the nephew of famed Russian exile, Leon Trotsky.

The investigation revealed that "Dr. Trotsky" had stayed several days at the Cortez Hotel during the same time the Fromes were there, and as noted, a pair of physician's thin rubber gloves was found near the crime scene.

Further, his physical description [Male, 40, 5-10, 162, black hair] generally fit that of the dark-haired man seen with the Fromes in Juarez, Mexico.

Trotsky had an extensive arrest record, which dated back some twenty years that included: murder [convicted of performing an abortion] and numerous petty thefts by trick and device. Trotsky was a well-established con man who regularly made outlandish claims such as being the "nephew of Leon Trotsky" [proven untrue] and used at least half a dozen alias in his cons.

A statewide *All Points Bulletin* was put out for his arrest, and Trotsky was located and detained in San Angelo, Texas on April 29, 1938. He was able to provide authorities with a solid alibi and was released from custody in short order, with no evidence to connect him to the Frome murders.

Even the most famous unsolved murders eventually grow old and cold, and after several months of front-page headlines, so it was with the *Frome Mesquite Murders* of Nancy and Hazel Frome.

After several decades, even the memory of this horrific crime faded from the public and only a few old school Texas Rangers recalled the details. In the Seventies, a young Texas Ranger by the name of H. Joaquin Jackson was assigned the thirty-year-old unsolved, based on a snitch, who provided the name of a "possible suspect." That lead took Ranger Jackson to Los Angeles where, with the help of two LAPD Robbery/Homicide Division detectives, he located the "suspect" who was living in L.A. The man denied any knowledge or involvement, provided an alibi, and passed a polygraph. Jackson would later write a book, *One Ranger Returns* (*University of Texas Press*, 2008) which includes a chapter on his cold-case investigation of the Frome Murders, concluding, "It's my opinion that all the witnesses and suspects, in this case, are deceased."

In January 2014, I received an Email from one of my readers, a Mr. Ron Dawson, who backgrounded me on the Texas Frome murders, of which I was totally unfamiliar. Having read my books and being familiar with my father's M.O., he suggested I look at the unsolved crime.

Here is Ron's Email as initially received:

January 4, 2014,

Dear Mr. Hodel,

We corresponded by email a couple of years ago. I was researching the unsolved murders of Hazel and Nancy Frome in late March 1938, west of El Paso. I was struck by the similarities with the Black Dahlia case. I put it on the shelf as was busy with other things, but now am continuing my research. I am enclosing an article from the Gallup (NM) Independent, Mar. 12, 1938, showing Dr. Hodel leaving his post there with the public health service and being reassigned to Santa Fe. There is also a puzzling ad in the Albuquerque Tribune where he is selling a 1937 Cadillac V-12 convertible coupe for $175. This was Feb. 6, 1938.

Both Gallup and Santa Fe are within a 5 or 6-hour drive to El Paso. In the late thirties, drugs were readily available across the bridge in Juarez, Mexico.

The Frome women, mother, and daughter were driving a 1938 Packard from Berkeley, Calif. to South Carolina to visit a married daughter, wife of a Marine. They had car trouble in El Paso and stayed at the Cortez Hotel for five days (March25-30) while the car was being repaired. It was noted that they frequently went to Juarez for clubs and dancing. They left on March 30, and 120 miles west of El Paso were abducted, tortured, and murdered. The daughter had evenly spaced cigarette burns on her hand. The mother had a chunk of flesh, apparently bitten from her arm.

It is interesting that on the same week that the women were at the Cortez, there was a public health conference at the same hotel. I have unsuccessfully tried to find the old hotel registers.

Just an update. Hope you are well.
Ron Dawson

I thanked him for the information and though skeptical that my father would be involved in a Texas case, a state that as far as I knew, he had never been to, nevertheless, I began researching and familiarizing myself with the 1938 case.

First, I reviewed most of the original newspaper articles and was amazed at just how "high profile" it was. The reportage equaled or may have even surpassed, the coverage of our own infamous "Black Dahlia" murder, a decade later. Next, I ordered and read Ranger Jackson's chapter on his own investigation of the case and followed up with an Email, providing him with details on my father's serial crime signatures.

I then made personal contact by phone, and we exchanged information and ended with me requesting to have Ranger Jackson contact the Austin, DPS to see if he could ascertain if any of the original evidence was still available for potential DNA analysis. He doubted that anything remained but agreed to see what he could discover. (No word back as of this writing.)

Then, just two months later, one of those amazing synchronistic events happened.

A veteran journalist/author, Clint Richmond, came out with a new true-crime book entitled, *Fetch the Devil: The Sierra Diablo Murders and Nazi Espionage in America. (ForeEdge Publishers 2014)*

A teaser for the new publication reads:

"*Fetch the Devil* is the first narrative account of this [Frome] still the officially unsolved case. Using long-forgotten archives and recently declassified FBI files, Clint Richmond paints a convincing portrait of a sheriff's dogged investigation into a baffling murder, the international spy ring that orchestrated it, and America on the brink of another world war."

I immediately ordered a copy and devoured it in two days. The author's sourcing and footnotes were immaculate and extensive. His dealing with the Texas DPS was a mirror image of my own attempts to obtain records and work with LAPD on the Dahlia case.

In his epilog, author Richmond writes that he made three separate attempts through the *FOIA* (*Freedom of Information Act*).

His first was in 1992, which was "denied." DPS claimed it was "an open case." His second request came in 1995, through his use of the "Texas Open Records Act" which was also, "denied." In 2006, the journalist made his third attempt requesting, "to examine the case files for historical research." Texas DPS responded with, "The records are gone." Richmond followed-up with additional inquiries and was finally informed, "The records have been shredded." No date of destruction was provided.

Finally, the storm passed, the clouds moved out, and the hot Texas sun broke through. In his 'Acknowledgments' Richmond writes:

> The most important contribution to never-before-published information in *Fetch the Devil* came from a dusty warehouse. The late sheriff of El Paso, Leo Samaniego, and his administrative deputy at the time, Sergeant

Jose Dominguez, responded to my Texas Open Records Act request by unearthing what is probably the only complete case file of the historic files of the historic Frome murders still in existence, since the unfortunate destruction of case files once held by the Texas Department of Public Safety.

Author Richmond's persistence paid off big-time. Shades of my own discovery of the secret *LADA Hodel-Black Dahlia Case Files,* which like these Frome Files, *had been* locked away from the public for more than fifty years.

Thanks to Richmond's surprising discovery of El Paso Sheriff Chris Fox's case file, [recall he was the original "coordinator" assigned to oversee the Frome investigation] we now have direct evidence from percipient witness statements, sourced from the official law enforcement reports. Thanks to Richmond's dedication and perseverance, we can rest assured that my recreated victim chronology is accurate and reliable.

Did Dr. George Hill Hodel Commit the Frome Torture Murders in 1938?

My short answer is—I think so. The circumstantial evidence that I am about to present, I believe you will find is strong and compelling.

However, absent DNA analysis of my father's full-profile [currently in my possession] to DNA obtained from the actual crime-scene evidence [which may or may not still exist] the case will remain officially unsolved.

We are now deeply backgrounded into all the known facts, witness observations and related physical evidence as presented in the previous day-by-day reconstruction of events leading up to the brutal torture-murders of Hazel and Nancy Frome on Wednesday, the 30th of March 1938.

Armed with that information, let us now examine the known history and movements surrounding the man I now believe could well be their killer—George Hill Hodel M.D.

Opportunity

The below excerpt is copied from George Hodel's 1945 application to join UNRRA (United Nations Relief and Rehabilitation Agency). It was personally prepared by my father, and in this section, he provides his work history for the years 1935-1945.

12. Give a brief résumé of your activities from time of graduation to the present time, including a statement of all positions which you have held, giving inclusive dates.

Intern, San Francisco County Hospital, 1935-36.
Camp Surgeon, CCC, New Mexico, Dec. 1936 - June 1937.
District Health Officer, Second Health District of New Mexico (County of McKinley and County of San Juan; headquarters, Gallup, New Mexico); Chief, McKinley County Venereal Disease Clinic; July 1937 - April 1938 (while health officer was on leave).
Social Hygiene Physician, Los Angeles County Health Department, in charge of venereal disease clinics at Santa Monica, Whittier, Compton, and East Los Angeles; May 1938 - January 1941.
Chief, Division of Social Hygiene, Los Angeles County Health Department, January 1941 to present.

After serving as the sole surgeon at a logging camp in New Mexico in 1936-1937, he was appointed the District Health Officer in the 2nd District [NW corner of New Mexico] and headquartered in Gallup, NM. Then he was named chief of the McKinley County Venereal Disease Clinic from July 1937 until April 1938, when he left the state and the following month became a Social Hygiene Physician for the L.A. County Health Department, in Los Angeles, California.

Here is an alarming piece of information from an article printed in the *Gallup Independent* dated January 17, 1938.

Apparently, a part of Dr. Hodel's duties as the State's District Health Officer included his serving as the Gallup NM, County Coroner.

This would require him to perform autopsies and establish whether the cause of death was the result of "natural cause" or the result of "foul play" and homicide.

Below we see the results of one of his examinations on the front page of the Gallup newspaper. According to Dr. Hodel, Mr. Morros died from, "natural causes."

..."Dr. G. Hill Hodel, District Health Officer attributed death to "natural causes, probably a heart attack." He [Hodel] said. "Mr. Morros had been dead several hours when the body was discovered early this morning."

Below we see Dr. George Hill Hodel's "For Sale" advertisement in the *Albuquerque Journal* for his 12-cylinder Cadillac that Ron Lawson mentioned in his original Email to me. No further information is known.

[SKH Note- $175.00 for this machine is definitely a "Depression" price-tag.]

Albuquerque Journal Feb 6, 1938

Alvarado Hotel

**CADILLAC V-12 Convertible Coupe 1937
One of the finest cars in New Mexico
$175. Call Dr. Hodel at the Alvarado Hotel
Sunday only.**

Photo (below) of Dr. George Hill Hodel treating a patient at the clinic in Santa Fe, New Mexico circa 1937-8.

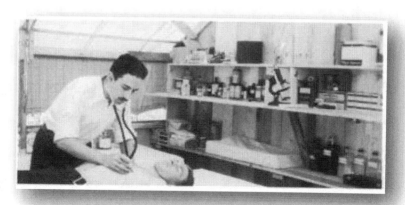

The following article appeared in the *Gallup Independent* newspaper on March 12, 1938 [Just eighteen days preceding the Fromes murder near Van Horn, Texas]. It announces the pending transfer of Dr. George Hodel by the *State Health Department* to Santa Fe, New Mexico from his current position as District Health Officer in Gallup, NM.

THE GALLUP INDEPENDENT
Saturday, March 12, 1938

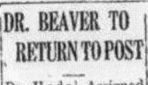

DR. BEAVER TO RETURN TO POST

Dr. Hodel Assigned To Santa Fe

Dr. C. S. Beaver, district health officer who has been on leave of absence, will return to Gallup Monday. Dr. G. Hill Hodel, who has been taking Dr. Beaver's place, is being assigned to Santa Fe, and will be loaned by the State Health Department to the Indian Service for a period of six months.

He will act as physician for the pueblos of San Ildefonso, Santa Clara, San Juan, Tesuque, and Nambe. Dr. Hodel's headquarters will be at the Charles Lummis hospital in Santa Fe.

Dr. Beaver, while on leave of absence, has been in private practice in Aztec. Before going on leave, he had been health officer here for two and a half years.

Characterizing McKinley county as an excellent field for public health work, Dr. Hodel expressed his appreciation of the way the community had cooperated in health department activities.

"In this district, people are acutely conscious of community health needs, and they have been interested and active in furthering our program. Civic organizations and public officials have shown a splendid community spirit in matters of health protection and improvement," Dr. Hodel said.

The distance from Santa Fe to El Paso is 328 miles and the driving time would have been approximately 4.5 hours. An easy day trip, on a par with the trip the Fromes, made their first day from San Francisco Bay area to Los Angeles.

While I have yet to be able to independently confirm his statement, let us recall Ron Dawson's statement to me in his original Email of January 4, 2014:

"...It is interesting that on the same week that the women were at the Cortez, there was a public health conference at the same hotel. I have unsuccessfully tried to find the old hotel registers."

The original Hotel Cortez is long gone now, and so are its records. However, the possibility remains that the names of all registrants could have been recorded by Sheriff Chris Fox and preserved in his case files.

Also, if in fact, there was a medical conference at the Cortez during that same week, I would expect that the probability is high that Dr. George Hodel would have made the short trip from Santa Fe, perhaps even as one of the presenters at the conference? This could also explain the reason why "Dr. Trotsky" was registered and stayed at the hotel during that same week, even though financially, the five-star hotel was "out of his league." Hoping to meet "fellow physicians," work the rooms, and try to drum up business would be a strong motive to be there for the experienced con-artist.

The Suspect Description

Most of the descriptions of the male seen with the Fromes both in Juarez at the nightclubs and later in El Paso, waiting for her outside the beauty salon were consistent with George Hodel's physical description. In 1938 George Hodel's physical description was a follows:

Male, 31 years, 6,' 165, coal black hair, dark brown eyes, and a mustache. He was an exceptionally dapper dresser and generally wore a business suit and fedora.

Photo of Dr. George Hill Hodel circa 1937

Witness Frances Hammer, who claimed to have obtained a close look at the suspect, provided the following description, which seems to stick with the newspaper that ran with it:

"Male with a sharp chin, prominent nose, and wearing a light-colored fedora hat, a dark coat, and a tan shirt. He had piercing dark eyes and looked like a dope fiend. I know about dope. I'm a nurse."

Two later photos of George Hodel: 1 & 1a) during

his 1949 court trial for child molestation and incest. 2) his 'book-in' 'mug shot' taken after his arrest for child molestation and incest.

"Dark piercing eyes"? You be the judge.

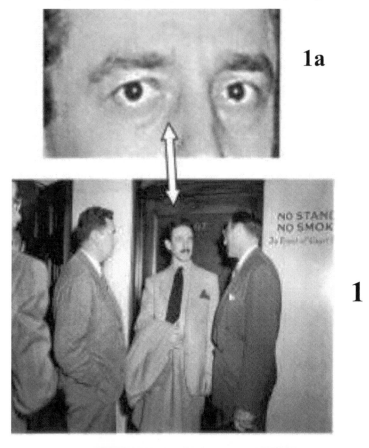

1a

1

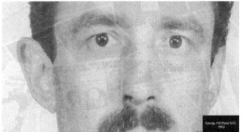

2

The Suspect Vehicle

We know that the suspects [two males and a female] were driving a black or dark-colored vehicle that whether it was a sedan or coupe, was smaller in size that the Frome's 1937 Packard 7-seater. Several separate witnesses said it had two license plates on it. One, a Texas license was "flapping in the wind," which could indicate it was possibly a temporary plate, loosely placed on the vehicle and possibly even stolen? The Greyhound bus driver, Mr. Harmon, spotted three suspects in the black sedan [two males and one female] and observed two plates on the rear "one possibly Texas and *the other was a New Mexico license plate.*" [Emphasis mine.]

The most distinctive vehicle description came from witness Jim Milam, who clearly stated that the suspect's vehicle had "white letters within a white border on the car's passenger door", but being illiterate, he could not read the writing. On his later sighting, he saw lettering on the vehicle's driver's door.

Witness Frances Hammer also confirmed seeing markings on the door panel and described them as "similar to the shield seen on a California Highway Patrol vehicle."

[SKH Note- The "shield" on a CHP patrol car was then, and remains to this day, the Great Seal of the State of California.]

1939 California Highway Patrol Car Markings

State Calif   State New Mexico

I would suggest the possibility that the markings and letters seen on the door panel of the suspect vehicle, by the three separate witnesses, on different occasions are consistent with what may have been an official New Mexico State Department of Health Department vehicle. [And may look similar to CHP markings above]

I am currently attempting to locate and identify such a vehicle, but, to my mind, it is highly likely that the State of New Mexico had their own official vehicles which would be marked with the State Seal and contain signage on the door panels, identifying it as such. Perhaps it included words to the effect, "New Mexico Health Department" or "NM District Health Officer, Official Business."

[Author's recreation: how vehicle *may* have appeared.]

Below is a photograph of a New Mexcio State "Official" car with its 1938 license plate. (plate number is fabricated)

The Physical Evidence

Earlier we reviewed a list of the various items of evidence that were recovered from or near the crime scene and that were then sent to the crime lab in Austin, Texas.

Let's consider a few of these items individually:

The **spent slugs** were from a .38 and a .32 and with three suspects involved, I believe it is safe to assume that two separate guns were used, fired execution style at point blank range to the heads. George Hodel both previous to and after 1938 used both caliber weapons in his separate serial murders.

The *"physician's rubber gloves* found wrapped inside California newspaper" are of particular interest for obvious reasons. We also know that Sheriff Chris Fox had a doctor/suspect [Dr. Trotsky] high on his list as the possible killer, put out an APB on him, and had him arrested as a POI. [Person of Interest] If these gloves still exist as evidence, they could well solve the case through "Touch DNA" with the potential of obtaining skin cells from the inside of the gloves and comparing it to the known DNA profile of Dr. George Hodel, currently in my possession.

It would also be of interest to examine the "California newspapers" evidence to establish where and when they were printed. Were they from Los Angeles or Berkeley? If L.A., did they correspond with the Fromes overnight stay on March 23-24, 1938, or could they have come from one of George Hodel's frequent trips to his "hometown"? We know from George Hodel's UNRRA application *that within just three weeks following the Frome murders* he had left his position as District Health Officer in New Mexico and relocated back to Los Angeles, where he hired on as a physician with the *Los Angeles County Health Department.* Was it just too hot in the desert?

The **"patch of black hair"** found clutched in Nancy Frome's hand, [if the follicles still exist] would also very likely produce positive DNA for comparison.

Obviously, the color is consistent with that of Dr. George Hill Hodel's hair.

The **man's handkerchief** also found grasped in Nancy Frome's right hand is, for me, of major significance. Why?

In at least four (4) of George Hodel's murders, that followed this crime into the 1940s, *a man's handkerchief was found near the victim's body.* As summarized in *Black Dahlia Avenger* [2006] and *Black Dahlia Avenger II* [2014] I name those victims in their separate murder investigations as: Suzanne Degnan (Chicago, 1946), Jeanne French (Los Angeles, 1947), Marian Newton (San Diego, 1947) and Gladys Kern (Los Angeles, 1948).

I also believe I have an answer as to why the handkerchiefs were left at the crime scenes.

Most likely, they were used as an aid to quickly silence the victim by my father using CHLOROFORM. The

M.O. was quick and simple and sure to work. A bottle of chloroform would literally be "on hand" carried in his doctor's bag, which obviously would be with him on all occasions. All he needed to do was just remove the bottle, pour it into his handkerchief and hold it firmly over the mouth and nose of his victim.

Chloroform drugging is almost unheard of in modern criminal investigations; however, the M.O. was quite common throughout the 1920s and 1930s.

In fact, it was so familiar, that we see it occur in many old movies, including the 1935 RKO film, The *Mysterious Mr. Wong*, starring Bela Lugosi and Wallace Ford. In that film, which was released just two years before the Frome murder, we see the suspect uses chloroform as his preferred method, to drug and then kidnap his victim.

Admittedly, I am an *old-school* detective, however, not *that old,* and not at all familiar with the use and effects of chloroform, so I decided to educate myself and contacted someone who was.

Below is my original email to my friend, Dr. Doug Lyle, along with his response. Doug as one of our nation's foremost forensic experts has appeared nationally and provided his expertise in many television shows, was a former consultant for Law & *Order* and is the author of numerous publications such as *Forensics for Dummies* [2004].

My Email to Dr. Doug:

Mon, Jun 16, 2014, at 9:39 PM Hi Doug:

Trust all goes well.

Can you give me your opinion and insights/knowledge as relates to the use of chloroform as a drug used for the primary purpose of assisting in the abduction and drugging of victims?

It is my belief that in many of my father's kidnappings and subsequent murders he used a handkerchief soaked with chloroform to initially help subdue his victims, all of whom I believe were females.

In at least five of his crimes "a man's handkerchief" was found near the body, which was usually posed in an isolated vacant lot, field or city sidewalk.

Keeping in mind that he was an M.D, had his medical bag with him on almost all occasions, and that this was a not an uncommon method used in the 20s and 30s, here are a few questions:

1) If the suspect walked up and grabbed and placed the soaked handkerchief over his victim's face, how long would

you estimate before she would either stop fighting her assailant and or become unconscious?

2) How long would the initial effects usually last? Would the victim remain unconscious or semi-conscious for minutes or longer? Half hour?

3) I assume a prescription was required to obtain the drug, and it was not "over the counter" even back then? Yes?

4) What kind of testing would be required to establish the presence of chloroform on the handkerchief back then? Would traces remain only for a short period or could the molecules be found through forensics even now five or more decades later? Spectrograph?

5) Assuming the handkerchief was held forcefully over the victim's mouth, would you think DNA might be present even decades later? Touch DNA?

6) Any other insights in general that you might think of as relates to this M.O.

Mucho Gras Amigo. Steve

Dr. Lyle's quick and expert response came the following day:

Tue, Jun 17, 2014, at 9:16 AM,

Steve

Chloroform works very quickly but is a short-acting anesthetic agent. If a soaked cloth was clapped over a victim's mouth and nose the drug would take effect very quickly--depending on how much was used and how effectively it covered the victim's face. The victim could lose consciousness in anywhere from 20-30 seconds and up to a couple of minutes. Then the effects could last anywhere from 10-30 minutes.

The actual time frame would depend on the dose given. And of course, if the cloth was left on too long and the victim OD'd on chloroform, she would stop breathing and die from asphyxia.

Drugs such as this were less well controlled in the 1930s as compared to now. Opium, Codeine, chloroform, and other drugs were relatively easy to come by---especially for a physician. So he would have no problem having it available.

Chemical testing of the cloth would likely reveal the chloroform--but maybe not. It could have gone either way back then. Whether it could still be found, decades later is a maybe yes and maybe no proposition also.

Yes, DNA could easily be picked up by the cloth as skin cells were wiped any and retained by the cloth. And yes they could still have usable DNA--or not--again it can go either way. But if the cloth was allowed to dry and then was stored in a cool place away from the elements, washing machines, etc. there could still be DNA present.

Hope this helps. Doug

The Frome Luggage

After deputies located the Frome Packard, they discovered that much of the **expensive luggage was missing**. I have yet to find any record that it was ever subsequently recovered. Since robbery appears not to have been a motive for the crime, **the suspects may have taken it to search through the Fromes' personal effects for the package and or letter that was received at the hote**l. These items if found by authorities **could contain** incriminating **evidence, potentially linking** one or more of the **killers to the victims**.

The Frome Killer's Signatures

Speaking as a homicide detective who has conducted over three hundred separate murder investigations, spanning a time period of more than fifty years, I cannot overstate how extremely rare and unique are the crime-signatures found in the Frome double homicide.

Especially, considering this crime occurred some eighty-one years ago.

This was not an isolated, one-time opportunistic crime, but was committed by a highly sophisticated sadist. A psychopath whose motive was not to rob or rape, but rather came from his pure enjoyment of inflicting absolute terror and pain upon his victims.

Also, *we are not here speculating* as to whether George Hodel was capable of committing such acts.

We know and have proven he was and did. Here is a list of documented crime-signatures, *separate from and not including the Frome signatures* that George Hodel, sometimes alone, sometimes with an accomplice, inflicted upon his victims during his reign of terror in the years and decades following the 1938 Frome murders. Judge for yourself:

~ Physical abduction of a female victim in her car from a public street
~ The use of a man's handkerchief (probably to chloroform victim) leaves handkerchief near the body

at the scene
~ Ligature strangulation
~ Severe beating about the face and head using a tire-iron or other blunt instrument
~ Dragging victim from the vehicle and careful posing of the body in an isolated area
~ Cuttings to extremities, arms and legs, and overall body premortem.
~ Slow torture, inflicting cigarette or cigar burns to the victim's body premortem.
~ Well dressed and dapper, approaches unknown female at a nightclub and asks her to dance, woos and invites her out "to see the town." Drives to an isolated area where he then beats her to death and poses body. [Two separate incidents one in L.A. and one in San Diego]
~ Uses handguns of different calibers on separate murders including .9mm, .38 and .32.
~ Sexual assault, performing sodomy with a foreign object on some victims, others left sexually unmolested, but with severe beating about the face and head with a tire iron or another object to inflict blunt force trauma. [Overkill]
~ After removing clothing has victim lay on the ground and stomps her torso with his foot so severely that it causes the ribs to puncture her heart.
~ After murder removes female clothing [all or partial] and carefully poses victim's body in both isolated and well-traveled public locations. [Golf Course, Residential and Business districts, Public Park, Sea-Side bluff, etc.]

Here is an on-point excerpt from my previous true-crime book, *MOST EVIL* (Dutton 2009) page 280:

...

In 2001, forensic psychiatrist Dr. Michael Stone of Columbia University developed a depravity scale from 1 to 22 to help courts rank heinous, atrocious, and cruel behavior. Category 1 includes those who kill in self-defense. At the bottom of the scale, Category 22 is reserved for the "most evil—psychopathic torturer-murderers with torture as their primary motive.

In September 2007, on the Discovery Channel's program entitled *Most Evil,* Dr. Stone ranked my father, Dr. George Hodel in Category 22.

Clip from one-hour television show *Most Evil* [2007]

22 GEORGE HODEL
PSYCHOPATHIC/ TORTURE-MURDER /
SERIAL KILLER / SEXUAL HOMICIDE

I quote from Dr. Stone's on-air observations:

"George Hodel was a deeply disturbed man, who although brilliant, had a twistedly distorted sense of reality. We have every reason to believe George Hodel enjoyed the horrible murder of Elizabeth Short and that he had took pleasure in what he had done for the rest of his long life. ...I would place George Hodel at the very top of my scale—level 22, psychopathic torture murders, with torture their primary motive."

Conclusion

Based on the accumulation of evidence, clearly we have made a strong, and compelling case that Dr. George Hill Hodel, very likely, committed the horrific double murders of Nancy and Hazel Frome, in the afternoon hours, on Wednesday, March 30, 1938.

I believe we have established the textbook axiom for, "MOM" satisfying, the "**M**ethod, the **O**pportunity, and the **M**eans."

If the physical evidence exists and can be tested for DNA–the potential for official clearance exists.

If documentation can be found, either from the Cortez Hotel records, or from El Paso Sheriff Chris Fox's original files to establish that Dr. George Hill Hodel, in fact, attended a March 1938, medical conference or was a registered guest at the hotel at the time of the murder, that would strengthen the case.

Finally, there remains the suspect vehicle. **Does a photograph exist of a New Mexico Health Department** (or other) **NM state car showing signage with** or without **a state seal** as I suspect? As suggested, the case could have turned on it's identification. Remember, (excerpt from page 22*)*, **Milam... noted the distinctive white lettering on the driver's doo**r, but acknowledged to authorities that he "was illiterate, *and could not read the writing written on the door panel."*

If any reader has or knows of such a photograph, please contact me.

I will continue to pursue all of these areas in hopes of adding to the weight of evidence.

Eighty-Year-Old 'THOUGHTPRINTS"
Some Dramatic Discoveries

In 2015, I conducted some research to verify my father's graduation information from medical school.

I was under the impression that he graduated from the UCSF Parnassus Campus in San Francisco and wrote the school to verify that as fact.

Assisted by a campus librarian I was able to obtain the actual commencement publication for the Class of '36 and discovered that the graduation actually took place on May 23, 1936. (cover page below)

UNIVERSITY OF CALIFORNIA

THE SEVENTY-THIRD
COMMENCEMENT

MAY, 1936

MAY 23

CALIFORNIA MEMORIAL STADIUM

BERKELEY

However, the ceremonies were not held at the medical school campus, but rather, at the then relatively new, *California Memorial Stadium* built at the foot of the Berkeley hills just a dozen years earlier. (1923)

California Memorial Stadium, Berkeley, aerial photo courtesy of NASA

I obtained a copy of my father's Class of '36 Commencement ceremonies and verified that yes, he had attended and received his M.D. on May 23, 1936. Below is a scan from the original program.

The Degree of Doctor of Medicine (Medical School) upon

Joseph Gilbert Hamilton (B.S. 1929)..Santa Barbara
G Kenneth Hargrove (A.B. 1932)...Berkeley
Joseph Hittelman (A.B. 1932)..Los Angeles
➡ George Hill Hodel (A.B. 1932)...South Pasadena
Wayne Stanford Hume (A.B. University of California at Los Angeles 1930)
                                                                                                    Pasadena

The Class of '36 Commencement included hundreds of graduating students not only from Parnassus medical school but also those graduating from U.C. Berkeley, where George Hodel had taken his pre-med courses. (1928-1932)

Listed under "Bachelors and Letters of Science" was the name–**Nancy Eudora Frome!**

Nancy Frome received a BS in Philosophy *and graduated along with George Hodel at the California Memorial Stadium on the same day–May 23, 1936.*

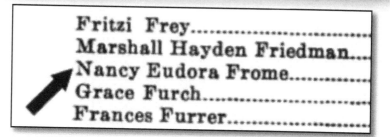

Bachelors—Letters and Science		29
Fritzi Frey	Latin	Rio Vista
Marshall Hayden Friedman	Zoölogy	Los Angeles
Nancy Eudora Frome	Philosophy	Berkeley
Grace Furch	German	San Francisco
Frances Furrer	History	Oakland
William Junji Furuta	Medical Sciences	Danville
² Kathryn Gable	English	Esparto
Ralph Warren Gaines	Political Science	Oakland
Mary Galbraith	French	Ash Grove, Missouri
¹ John J Gallagher	Political Science	Berkeley

Fritzi Frey.....................
Marshall Hayden Friedman.....
Nancy Eudora Frome.............
Grace Furch.....................
Frances Furrer..................

U.C. Berkeley May 23, 1936, Commencement Program listing graduation of Nancy Frome.

Less than two years later, while on a touring trip with her mother through El Paso, she would meet "an unidentified 'prior acquaintance' from California" and have dinner and drinks in Juarez, Mexico.

Mother and daughter after receiving a sealed letter addressed to "Frome" and left at their hotel that same evening would become fearful and the following morning would suddenly check out of their El Paso hotel. After a brief attempt at the adjacent travel agency to try and hire a male passenger to accompany them to Dallas (obviously for protection purposes), they would quickly depart downtown El Paso in their now repaired Packard and continue their road trip. Witness statements show they were chased by "two men and a woman," stopped by them on the highway, kidnapped from their car, and then brutally tortured and murdered.

Continuing my search, I discovered a second name listed at the graduation, that of **William Crawford, Nancy's Frome's 1936 fiancée**, who would, less than two years later, become a major witness in the Fromes murder investigation.

University of California – Berkeley
May 23, 1936
Commencement Program
Listing graduation of
Doctor William Crawford

CURRICULUM IN OPTOMETRY

Certificate of Completion to

Julieta Elvira Arias	David, Republic of Panama
Arthur Chong	San Rafael
[1] Max Budge Cole	Oakland
William Crawford	Turlock
Lawrence Halsey Foster	San Jose
Richard Fowler	Phoenix, Arizona
Arthur Joseph Gay	Berkeley

William Crawford graduated on the same day at the same ceremony as George Hodel with a doctorate in Optometry. At the time he was the fiancé of Nancy Frome. In the summer of '37, just one year later, Nancy would return his ring to him and break off their engagement.

Dr. Crawford would open a practice in San Francisco and marry another woman.

Crawford, as the former fiancée of Nancy Frome, became an important *interview* witness for authorities shortly after the double homicide in 1938.

Before Tragedy Struck

Miss Nancy Frome is shown with her parents, Mr. and Mrs. Weston G. Frome, in a picture snapped after her University of California graduation. Mother and daughter were slain in Texas.

Photo with her parents taken on May 23, 1936, at Nancy Frome's commencement at Memorial Stadium in Berkeley.

A check of 1932 residential records showed that George Hodel resided at 1427 Oxford Street, in Berkeley. Nancy Frome lived at her parents' home, 2560 Cedar Street, also in Berkeley. The distance between the two homes *was just one-half mile--five city blocks*

Engagement of
Miss Nancy Eudora Frome
Announced

Published announcement reads:

"Miss Nancy Eudora Frome of Berkeley, Calif., whose engagement to Mr. William Crawford of Turlock, Calif., has been announced by her parents, Mr. and Mrs. W.G. Frome of Berkeley, formerly of Joplin.

Both Miss Frome and her fiancé are graduates of the University of California. The wedding will take place in April."

February 28.1937

Map shows that in 1932 George Hodel and Nancy Frome lived only five-city blocks from each other. Both attended UC Berkeley and shared graduation exercises on May 23, 1936. Their commencement ceremony was held at the California Memorial Stadium, Berkeley as shown on the map.

We recall that one of the witnesses in the 1938 Fromes murder investigation, a Mr. B.N. Gist, while seated at a nearby table next to the Fromes at the *Café Juarez, in Juarez Mexico, had seen two men approach the mother and daughter. He recalled the two men had their "hats in hand" and overheard the conversation believed to come from Mrs. Frome, that she was "sure she had seen or met one of the men on the Pacific Coast."*

The two men, "polite and well dressed" then invited the women to join them across the street at the Tivoli Café.

Witness Gist was unsure if the ladies, after finishing their drinks, accepted the men's invitation and joined the two strangers or not?

Was this the link to George Hodel? Did my father know either the mother and or the daughter from Berkeley, California? Had they, living just blocks apart, met during Nancy's school years, or at a social function?

We have now established as fact that George Hill Hodel and Nancy Frome lived only five city blocks apart and attended the same commencement ceremonies together at the Oakland Stadium. Nancy received her Bachelor of Science degree and George receiving his Medical Degree.

This simply cannot be "coincidence."

While it may have been a "chance meeting" in Juarez, Mexico and at the Cortez Hotel in El Paso, Texas, yet these newly discovered facts establishing that George Hodel lived just blocks away from the Fromes, along with the fact that he attended the same graduation ceremonies with the murder victim, Nancy Frome provides us with a significant link, of the suspect to the victim, that was hitherto unknown.

Photo from Acme News pictures San Francisco Bureau
dated 4/7/38. Back of photo reads:

GRIEF-STRICKEN KIN FOLLOW MURDERED
WOMEN'S CASKETS

BERKELEY, California—The final parting of the Frome Family: the caskets of Mrs. Frome and HER DAUGHTER, Nancy being taken into a local mausoleum, after services following their brutal murders in a lonely Texas area. Following the caskets are the surviving members of the family. Weston Frome, husband, and father is supported by his son-in-law and daughter, Lieut. R.L. McMakin and wife.

THE AFTERMATH

This investigation of the 1938 double homicide of Hazel and Nancy Frome was originally intended to be included as the last chapter in a yet to be published book, tentatively titled, *Dr. George Hill Hodel 'The Early Years'* which will present the serial crimes believed committed by my father, Dr. George Hill Hodel, spanning two decades—the 1920s and 1930s.

At the time of this writing, those serial crimes number approximately fifteen and were all committed within the State of California. "The Early Years" investigation is ongoing.

Those unique M.O.'s and crime signatures will, when published, offer further proofs and support in corroboration to this investigation.

The West Texas Mesquite Murders, of Hazel and Nancy Frome were committed *just two weeks prior* to George Hodel leaving his job as District Health Officer with the New Mexico State Health Department.

My investigation so far would indicate that this West Texas double homicide was the last known serial crime George Hodel committed out of state, before relocating back to his city of birth, Los Angeles.

He joined the L.A. County Health Department as a social hygiene physician, in May 1938.

As presented in *Black Dahlia Avenger* (Arcade 2003, updated in Skyhorse Publications 2015) and its sequel, *Black Dahlia Avenger II* (Thoughtprint Press 2014, updated in *Black Dahlia Avenger III* (Rare Bird Books 2018) George Hodel's Los Angeles abductions and killings, resumed in what I have named the *Los Angeles Lone Woman Murders.*

Those thirteen crimes began with the abduction and brutal overkill murder of Mrs. Ora Murray in July 1943 (whose body he posed on an isolated golf course) and continued through February 1950 with the felony assault and probable murder of a "Jane Doe" victim.

That victim's assault occurred in the basement of Doctor George Hodel's then Hollywood residence, the Sowden/Franklin House, was overheard and recorded by DA and LAPD detectives on secret police surveillance wire recordings.

The stakeout officers from LAPD and LADA while listening to the crime and hearing and recording the blows to the body and the woman's screams in real time were just three miles away, in the basement of Hollywood Division Police Station—*took no action.* Consequently, the victim was never identified, nor was the crime ever formally reported, and remained unknown until the discovery of the secret transcripts some fifty-three years later.

Law enforcement's (LADA and LAPD) six-week electronic stakeout of Dr. Hodel's private Hollywood residence in February and March of that year resulted in their obtaining recorded admissions to a number of his murders.

These confessions included the brutal torture-murder of Elizabeth "Black Dahlia" Short as well as his admitted forced overdose of his personal clinic secretary, Ruth Spaulding with whom he was having an ongoing affair. Also discovered on the electronic recordings were his confessions to "payoffs to police" and "performing abortions, lots of them."

Based on new information discovered in 2018 which included an original and hitherto unknown paid police informant letter written by a Mr. W. Glenn Martin on October 26, 1949 (fully summarized in the Afterword Chapter of *Black Dahlia Avenger III* (Rare Bird Books 2018) we now know and have documented evidence that Dr. George Hodel was actively being investigated by LAPD and taken in and "grilled by detectives" as a suspect on three separate murders.

Those three Los Angeles murders included: The May 1945 suspected forced overdose drugging murder of his secretary, Ruth Spaulding; the January 1947 murder of Elizabeth "Black Dahlia" Short, and the June 1949 abduction/torture murder of Mrs. Louise Springer.

George Hodel tipped, by Confederates, he was about to be arrested by LADA's Bureau of Investigation, fled the United States to avoid arrest and prosecution.

Important Author's Note

Absent the knowledge of "what came before, and after" the brutal double homicide of Hazel and Nancy Frome, readers would be justified in considering the linking of Dr. George Hill Hodel to the crimes that comprise *In The Mesquite* as "a bit of a stretch."

I intend to present the "what came before" ("The Early Years") in the relatively near future, perhaps a year or so more of investigation and linkage.

That said, the "what came after" is known and well-documented in my five previously published books on my father's life and crimes as well as in official LAPD and DA reports.

These many crimes (25 additional victims, in the 30 years following the Fromes double homicide) along with their unique MO's and crime-signatures as George Hodel's further serial murders, are very real evidence and further proofs connecting him to the earlier West Texas murders of Hazel and Nancy Frome.

<u>Here then, follows the</u>:

INTRODUCTION
OF THE

L.A. LONE WOMAN
AND
CHICAGO "LIPSTICK" MURDERS

A summary of those crimes
that span the years 1943-1969.
Judge for yourself.

THE

L.A. LONE WOMAN
AND
CHICAGO "LIPSTICK" MURDERS

In my investigation to date, I have attributed to my father, George Hill Hodel, twenty-five (25) murders, spanning the period of some twenty-five years (1943 to 1969). Victims photographs and dates of occurrence shown below.

The Victims: 1943-1969

These are crimes I had previously classified and documented as "Category I" murders — "Definites."

What follows is a chronological overview, identifying each one of my father's "Category I" crime victims by name, location, and the responsible investigative agency along with a brief synopsis of each crime.

The initial crimes (LA Lone Woman and Chicago Lipstick Murders) span the thirteen years from the time George Hodel left New Mexico in 1938 just weeks after the Fromes double homicide until he fled Los Angeles in the fall of 1950, as he was about to be arrested and charged by the DA's office for multiple LA murders.

1] ORA MURRAY—

"The White Gardenia Murder"

Los Angeles Sheriff's detectives at 1943 Ora Murray crime scene

Above is the gruesome scene at the Fox Hills Golf Club parking lot, where the semi-nude body of Mrs. Ora E. Murray was found last July 27.

ORA MURRAY—

"The White Gardenia Murder"

July 26, 1943, Los Angeles
(Los Angeles Sheriff's Department)

Victim, age forty-two, met suspect who introduced himself as "Paul from San Francisco" at a dance hall in downtown Los Angeles. Ora was invited out by Paul to "show her Hollywood." Driven to an isolated golf park, strangled, and savagely beaten with a tire iron causing severe blunt force trauma to her head and face.

The cause of death: "constriction of the larynx by strangulation and concussion of the brain and subdural hemorrhage."

Her killer ceremoniously draped a sarong over the victim's body and placed a white gardenia next to the body. What went unnoticed was that the suspect's crime had been patterned after a recent Suspense Theatre Hollywood radio play, *The White Rose Murders*, starring actress, Maureen O'Hara. The show had aired in Los Angeles on July 6, 1943, just twenty days before the killer's "reenactment." The slaying of victim Ora Murray was identical to the radio script, originally written by popular novelist/screenwriter, Cornell Woolrich.

2] GEORGETTE BAUERDORF—

"The Bathtub Murder"

1944 Bauerdorf investigation:
The note typed by killer was smeared with red medical antiseptic Mercurochrome to imitate blood. (Jack the Ripper used red ink to simulate blood in his mailings to press.)

GEORGETTE BAUERDORF—

"The Bathtub Murder"

October 11, 1944, Los Angeles
(Los Angeles Sheriff's Department)

The victim, age twenty, was followed home from the well-known Hollywood Canteen where she volunteered as a junior hostess, helping entertain servicemen during WWII. After gaining entry, Georgette was assaulted inside her apartment, beaten, asphyxiated by having a gag* forced down her throat. The cause of death was "obstruction of upper air passages by inserted cloth." Her killer then post-mortem carried her body to the bathroom, placed it inside the tub, and turned on the water. A witness in the building later in the morning heard the sound of running water and, in checking the apartment, found her body in the bathtub.

*(9"-wide piece of elastic-type medical bandage—see pages 201-204 for additional photos/info.)

Robbery not a motive as valuable jewelry and money were left behind; however, the suspect did take her car, which was found abandoned near downtown Los Angeles.

In 1945 on the one-year anniversary of the Bauerdorf slaying, her killer left a taunting typewritten note, later published in the newspapers, taking credit for her murder. He bragged he would "appear at the Hollywood Canteen in uniform on or about Oct. 11th." Further, he informed the public he had killed her due to "Divine Retribution—catch me if you can." Newspapers called this "The Bathtub Murder". LA Sheriffs actively investigated it as possibly being connected to several "Chicago Lipstick/Bathtub murders."

3] RUTH SPAULDING

LA County Coroner's Register

Listing Ruth Spaulding's "Probable Cause of Death, 'Barbital poisoning,' due to ingestion of lethal dose of barbiturates. Suicidal."

Incredibly, this coroner's document confirms

Dr. Hodel's electronic surveillance statement made nearly five years later, showing the coroner was notified of the death at 12:45 a.m., which would have been just six-minutes after she was pronounced dead at Georgia Street Receiving Hospital at 12:39 a.m

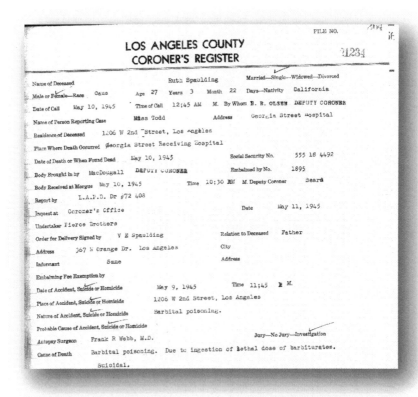

LOS ANGELES COUNTY
CORONER'S REGISTER

FILE NO. 21234

Name of Deceased	Ruth Spaulding	Married—Single—Widowed—Divorced
Male or Female—Race Caus	Age 27 Years 3 Month 22 Days—Nativity California	
Date of Call May 10, 1945	Time of Call 12:45 AM M. By Whom E. E. OLSEN DEPUTY CORONER	
Name of Person Reporting Case Miss Todd	Address Georgia Street Hospital	
Residence of Deceased 1206 W 2nd Street, Los Angeles		
Place Where Death Occurred Georgia Street Receiving Hospital		
Date of Death or When Found Dead May 10, 1945	Social Security No. 555 18 4492	
Body Brought in by MacDougall DEPUTY CORONER	Embalmed by No. 1895	
Body Received at Morgue May 10, 1945	Time 10:30 AM M. Deputy Coroner Beard	
Report by L.A.P.D. Dr #72 408		
Inquest at Coroner's Office	Date May 11, 1945	
Undertaker Pierce Brothers		
Order for Delivery Signed by V E Spaulding	Relation to Deceased Father	
Address 367 N Orange Dr. Los Angeles	City	
Informant Same	Address	
Embalming Fee Exemption by		
Date of Accident, Suicide or Homicide May 9, 1945	Time 11:45 P M.	
Place of Accident, Suicide or Homicide 1206 W 2nd Street, Los Angeles		
Nature of Accident, Suicide or Homicide Barbital poisoning.		
Probable Cause of Accident, Suicide or Homicide		
Autopsy Surgeon Frank R Webb, M.D.	Jury—No Jury—Investigation	
Cause of Death Barbital poisoning. Due to ingestion of lethal dose of barbiturates. Suicidal.		

RUTH SPAULDING

(Suspected Forced Overdose by Pills)

May 9, 1945, Los Angeles
(Los Angeles Police Department)

The victim, age twenty-seven, was single and lived alone in a downtown apartment in Los Angeles, California.

Victim employed as a personal secretary to Dr. George Hill Hodel at his *First Street Clinic*. Ms. Spaulding was having an ongoing sexual affair with Dr. Hodel, and they had "recently broken up."

Ruth had written several manuscripts and threatened to expose several of Dr. Hodel's known criminal activities. (These included false diagnosis to patients, illegal billings, performing abortions, etc.) Dr. Hodel on the pretense of "making up and getting back together" came to victim's apartment where he drugged (possibly by injection?) and forced her to ingest a lethal amount of sleeping pills.

After staging the "suicide," he then called his wife, Dorothy Hodel, to the scene, while the victim remained unconscious but still alive and breathing and gave her the incriminating manuscripts and ordered her to "take them and burn them." His wife complied.

Dr. Hodel remained in the apartment with the victim until she became comatose and at death's door, then transported her by taxi to Georgia Street Receiving Hospital where she was pronounced dead one hour later.

LAPD investigated the death as suspicious and "possible foul play," but their investigation was terminated nine months later, when Dr. Hodel left the country after joining UNRRA and going to China in February 1946.

Four years later, on the secret DA Hodel/Black Dahlia electronic recordings Dr. Hodel would be recorded admitting to overdosing and "killing his secretary" and expressing concern that "maybe they [police] have figured it out." He was also recorded stating, "**Supposin' I did kill the Black Dahliah.** [sic] **They couldn't prove it now. They can't talk to my secretary** [Spaulding] **anymore because she's dead**.

They [Georgia Street Receiving Hospital] pronounced her dead at 12:39."

Top of the next page: what looks like an abstract image in the middle of the picture is an artist's idea of the apaprtment's interior and movement of the killer.

The Chicago "Lipstick Murders"

4] JOSEPHINE ROSS—

Josephine Ross Apartment

Josephine Ross with daughter Jacqueline

JOSEPHINE ROSS—

June 3, 1945, Chicago, Illinois
(Chicago Police Department)

"The Bathtub Murder"
aka "The Lipstick Killer Murder."

The victim, age forty-three, was accosted in her apartment on Chicago's Northside, mid-morning shortly after having breakfast with her two daughters, who then left the shared apartment. The police investigation revealed her intruder entered the apartment and a violent struggle ensued. The victim was attacked with a knife and received defense wounds to her hand and thumb. She was then struck on the head with five powerful blows which likely rendered her unconscious.

The assailant stabbed her five times in the neck and severed her jugular vein, which was the cause of death.

When discovered, she was found holding several black strands of hair which she had pulled from her attacker's head during the struggle. The suspect then committed the following highly unusual acts postmortem:

1) He placed the victim's body in the bathtub and washed it clean using a douche bag found in the bathroom.
2) He towel-dried the body and carried it to the victim's bed.
3) Using strips of medical adhesive tape, he covered over the lacerations he had inflicted on her face.
4) He tied a woman's silk stocking tightly around her throat.

5) Finally, he draped a red skirt over her head.

A witness observed the suspect exit the apartment building using an exterior fire escape and provided the following description: "A tall male, thirty years, black wavy hair, wearing a light-colored sweater." (GHH was thirty-seven but could easily pass for younger.)

The Ross crime was later connected as one of the three "Lipstick Murders," but this one was initially known as "The Bathtub Murder." (As mentioned previously, Los Angeles sheriffs would investigate this as possibly connected to the Bauerdorf "Bathtub Murder" that occurred in LA just nine months prior.)

5] FRANCES BROWN—CLK

Killer's taunting message left on Brown's apartment wall, hence the Chicago Press' dubbing the crime: "The Lipstick Murder"

FRANCES BROWN—CLK "By Knife, By Gun"
December 10, 1945, Chicago, Illinois
(Chicago Police Department)
"The Bathtub Murders," "The Lipstick Killer Murder"

The victim, age thirty-three, had recently been working in Washington DC and was newly discharged from the US Navy WAVES. (Women Appointed for Voluntary Emergency Service).

This crime was identical in almost every respect to the murder of Josephine Ross, which occurred just six months prior and only one-quarter mile away. The knife-wielding suspect entered her apartment, approached her in her bedroom, and a struggle ensued and victim received multiple knife cut "defense wounds" to her hands. The suspect then stabbed the victim in the neck with a large bread knife which he had removed from the kitchen. In addition, she was shot twice, once in the right arm and a second time in the forehead, which caused instantaneous death. As in the Ross attack, the killer dragged her body to the bathroom and used a douche bag to wash the blood away. He then removed her pajamas and wrapped them around the bloody knife and left it embedded in her neck, leaving her posed in the tub. As a final taunting act, he went to the south living room of the apartment, removed a framed picture, placed it on the floor, and, using a lipstick tube, wrote in bright red letters ranging from three to six inches in size:

for heavens
sake catch me
Before I kill more
I cannot control myself

Chicago Tribune *dubs Brown's murderer,*
"The Lipstick Killer."

Miss Frances Brown, a former
WAVE, who was shot and stabbed
to death in her apartment on Dec.
10, 1945, by slayer who left macabre
message in lipstick on the wall.

Ex-Navy Wave, Frances Brown

Chicago PD investigation identified the murder weapon as a .38-caliber handgun. The suspect gained entry to the apartment by climbing an exterior fire escape and entering an open window. After turning the radio on loud, he exited through the front door.

The night manager observed the suspect in the hallway at approximately 4:00 a.m. and described him as: "Male Caucasian, thirty-five to forty years, dark complexioned wearing a dark overcoat and dark fedora hat."

A tenant who resided directly under the victim's apartment later reported hearing possible gunshots around 3:00 a.m. Several days after the murder, this witness received a threatening phone call from the possible suspect who stated, "I'm the lipstick killer. You'll get it next if you don't keep your mouth shut."

6] SUZANNE DEGNAN – CLK ------------>

Next page is the Assoicated Press' "'*NOTE*' (accompanying this picture in the papers) "*Here is one side of the note found in victim's room. It reads:*

"Get $20,000 reddy & waite for word do not notify F B I or police Bills in 5's and 10's."

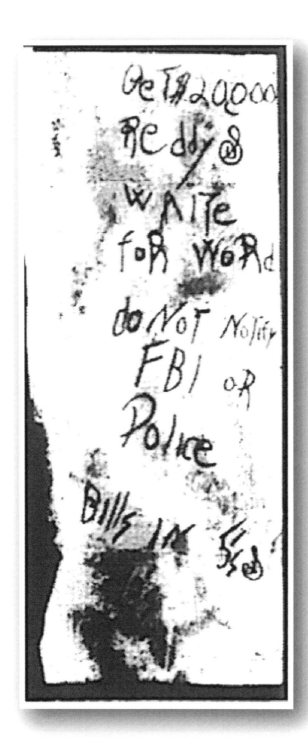

6] SUZANNE DEGNAN – CLK
"By Knife, By Rope"

January 7, 1946, Chicago, Illinois
(Chicago Police Department)
"The Lipstick Killer Murders"

The victim, age six, wearing pajamas, was asleep in a large family residence on Chicago's north side. She was abducted from her upstairs bedroom.

Police theorized a wooden ladder was used to possibly gain entry through a second-floor window.

A ransom note was left in the bedroom. The child was strangled to death and taken to the basement of a nearby apartment building where her body was surgically dismembered; the body parts washed clean, wrapped in paper and/or rags which the killer(s) placed in six separate nearby sewers.

After nearly a day of police searching for the kidnapped child, a man (likely her killer) called the family residence and suggested the police "search the storm drains in the neighborhood."

Police located what they described as "The Murder Room" (a basement) at 5901 Winthrop Avenue, just two city blocks from the victim's home.

Residents of this location admitted hearing noises, footsteps and running water at 3:00 a.m., but took no action.

On the following page is the text of the Degan ransom note that was left inside the victim's bedroom. The note written by the killer, feigning illiteracy, demanded $20,000 in small bills.

I believe that in committing this crime, Dr. George Hodel was paying homage to two of the world's most infamous crimes; those of Jack the Ripper and the 1932 kidnap-murder of the Lindbergh Baby. Why?

Because the MO similarities between Degnan and Lindbergh are too unique to simply call them "coincidences." It had to be deliberate. George Hodel was recommitting the Lindbergh kidnap, but unlike the suspect Richard Hauptmann (later arrested, tried, convicted, and executed), GHH would outwit the police and get away with his copycat crime, proving to the world that he was much smarter than his predecessor and truly in a class of his own as a master criminal.

Here are a few identical and unique MOs used in both the Lindbergh and Degnan crimes:

• Wealthy home in an upscale neighborhood selected

• Ladder used to gain entrance to child's second-floor bedroom

• Handwritten ransom note left in bedroom

• Feigns illiteracy note containing many spelling mistakes

This MO coupled with a side-by-side comparison of the wording in both notes, in my opinion, informs us that the Degnan case is a copycat crime to Lindbergh.

You Compare:

Degnan 1946 Ransom note
left in bedroom read:

*Get $20,000 reddy & waite for word do
not notify FBI or Police
Bills in 5's & 10's*

Burn this for her safty

Lindbergh 1932 Ransom note
left in bedroom read:

*Dear Sir!
Have 50.000$ redy 25 000$ in 20$bills
15000$ in 10$ bills and 10000$ in 5$ bills
After 2–4 days we will inform you were to
deliver the mony
We warn you for making anyding
public or for notify the Police
The child is in gut care.*

A second note: *written in lipstick* was found on a telephone pole outside and near the "Murder Room" on Winthrop Avenue.

It read:

*Stop
Me
Before
I
Kill
More*

Lipstick printed sign on post near building where body of Suzanne Degnan was dismembered, discovered yesterday.

Suzanne Degnan, age six
Degnan northside home | Degnan parents

January 8, 1946, *Chicago Tribune* "Jack the- Ripper-like headlines. The city will remain terrorized and in fear for many months following the Suzanne Degnan crime.

A third note, allegedly written by the "Lipstick Killer," was mailed to the Chicago police. In this note, the killer threatens to commit suicide. (In later Avenger and Zodiac mailings, the killer also publicly announced his intent to commit suicide). Also, like the earlier Bauerdorf typed letter to police, the writer claims he can be found at a specific location. Police went to the address but found no suspect.

> *Why don't you catch me. If you don't **ketch** me soon, I will **cummit** suicide. There is a reward out for me. How much do I get if I give myself up. When do I get that 20,000 dollars they wanted from that Degnan girl at 5901 Kenmore Avenue. You may find me at the Club Tavern at 738 E. 63rd St. known as Charlie the Greeks. Or at Conway's Tavern at 6247 Cottage Grove Au.*
>
> *Please hurry now.*

Chicago PD, in the months following these "Lipstick Killer" murders, was under tremendous pressure to solve the crimes. Citizen vigilante mobs were ready to move on anyone who even had the slightest suggestion of being a possible "suspect."

Multiple arrests (at least six) on different males were made oftentimes with heavy-handedness with the police using excessive force.

One elderly individual, Hector Verburgh, age sixty-five, who was employed as a janitor at the same Winthrop Avenue apartment where the Degnan girl was dismembered, was arrested, tortured, and hospitalized.

After his release a few days later without being charged, his attorney sued and won a large settlement from the City for police brutality. Mr. Verburgh, when interviewed by the press, had this to say:

> Oh, they hanged me up, they blindfolded me. I can't put up my arms; they are sore. They had handcuffs on me for hours and hours. They threw me in a cell and blindfolded me. They handcuffed my hands behind my back and pulled me up on bars until only my toes touched the floor. I no sleep, I no eat, I go to the hospital. Oh, I am so sick. Any more and I would have confessed anything.

William Heirens: "The Lipstick Killer"

On June 26, 1946, a seventeen-year-old, opportunist daytime burglar by the name of William Heirens entered an unlocked apartment, took a single dollar bill from a wallet on a dresser, and exited. On his person, he also had a gun taken in an earlier burglary. The teenage burglar was spotted by a witness and took off running.

An off-duty policeman chased him, fired several shots at him and Heirens took out the pistol and threw it at the pursuing officer.

A second officer gave chase and broke a flowerpot over Heirens' head. Heirens was arrested and booked for burglary.

Chicago PD detectives, figuring Heirens must have something to hide to flee from the police, though it was six months after the Degnan murder, decided to make Heirens the next "Lipstick Killer suspect."

Though still a juvenile, Heirens was deprived of sleep and food, grilled around the clock, beaten, prevented from speaking with an attorney or his parents, subjected to a spinal tap without anesthetic, and injected with sodium pentothal ("truth serum").

He had ether poured on his testicles and was given a lie detector test without his consent. (Though concealed for more than a decade, the results of that exam according to experts showed Heirens was telling the truth when he stated he did not kill Suzanne Degnan, Josephine Ross, or Frances Brown, the three "Lipstick Killer" victims.)

Teenager Bill Heirens being booked for Degnan murder after June 1946 arrest

In 1948, the City of Chicago agreed to settle Hector Verburgh's claim for wrongful arrest and police brutality for a sum of $20,000 (a considerable amount in 1948 dollars).

Chicago Daily Tribune
FINAL

HEIRENS FACES FATE TODAY

COURT HEARS EVIDENCE ON KILLER'S PLEAS *Ragen Quiz Up in Air; Widow Balks at 2d Autopsy*

Hint Threats by Gang Stall Slaying Probe

Admits His Guilt in 29 Crimes

THE NEW MOUNT

'COW COUNTRY' BITTER AT OPA, TURNS TO G.O.P.

U. S. Blamed by G.M. Head for Auto Lag

REVEALS F. D. R. 'GAVE' ROAD TO LATIN POLITICO

Secret War Deals

WEDNESDAY, SEPTEMBER 4, 1946.   FOURTEEN PAGES   FOUR CENTS

Heirens Pleads Guilty to Three Chicago Murders

Catfish?

Oklahoma City—Deputy U. S. Marshal Claude Street, discouraged by four days of unsuccessful fishing, returned home to mourn his luck.

From the back porch where he had left his tackle, he heard loud howls and rushed out to find his neighbor's cat, attracted by remnants of bait, hooked on one of the lines.

Court Hearings Opened to Fix His Punishment

Cases Are Reviewed After Halting Plea by College Youth

Pops by Proxy

Prescott, Ariz.—Edward C. Jordan of Oak Park, Ill., wanted to propose to Nancy Pratt, but he knew only that the Illinois girl was at a dude ranch near Prescott.

From Fort Wayne, Ind., yesterday, he called Prescott, telephone No. 1, which turned out to be in a furniture store, and told Gene Lloyd his romantic problem.

Action to Block Out McCarthy Is Turned Down

Zimmerman's Office Refuses Request From Appleton

Re: Photo on previous page:
"Heirens Faces Fate Today"

August 1946 Heirens is seen "Center Ring" in a legal circus attended by twenty "officials" (attorneys, Chicago police, arresting officers, detectives and sheriffs, all wanting to be present) when on the advice of his defense attorney Heirens is about to plead guilty to the "Lipstick Murders" to save himself from being executed. When asked by State's Attorney Tuohy (seated at the desk directly across from Heirens) if he is offering to plead guilty because "You are in fact guilty of these murders?" Heirens says, "No" and the meeting is quickly and unexpectedly adjourned to allow Heirens "to think it through." A month later in September, he will "cop a plea" to save his life, then recant it immediately after being transferred to the State Prison.

The evidence exonerating Heirens of the three "Lipstick Killer Murders" is overwhelming.

Too much to attempt to detail here, but for those interested, I recommend you read author and paralegal Dolores Kennedy's excellent book, *William Heirens: His Day In Court* (Bonus Books, Chicago 1991).

Dolores worked hand in hand with attorney Steve Drizen and his team at the Center on Wrongful Convictions at Chicago's Bluhm Legal Center, Northwestern University School of Law.

Judge Luther Swygert of the US Court of Appeals had this to say about the Heirens Case in 1968:

The case presents the picture of a public prosecutor and defense counsel, if not indeed the trial judge, buckling under the pressure of a hysterical and sensation-seeking press bent upon obtaining retribution for a horrendous act. The State's Attorney and defense counsel usurped the judicial function, complying with a community scheme inspired by the press to convict the defendant without his day in court.

In a notable book, *Your Newspaper: Blueprint for a Better Press* (MacMillan Co. 1947) written by Nine Nieman Fellows[5] the authors point directly to the many journalistic abuses employed by the *Chicago Tribune*, in that reportage of the Heirens investigation.

Here are a few Heirens-related excerpts from that book. Pages 48–50:

The Heirens murder story in Chicago illustrated how newspapers sometimes lose their sense of proportion. William Heirens, a seventeen-year-old University of Chicago sophomore, was arrested by Chicago police in June 1946 and held for questioning in connection with the kidnap-murder of six-year-old Suzanne Degnan and the murder of two women. Heirens denied knowing anything about the crimes.

5 The Nieman Foundation for Journalism is the primary journalism institution at Harvard. Founded in 1938, its stated goal is "to promote and elevate the standards of journalism in the United States and educate persons deemed specially qualified for journalism."

When he was held for the grand jury for assault and
burglary (not for murder), the four Chicago dailies
began to go to town, calmly and professionally, almost as
if the Degnan case were secondary to their circulation
war. The assigned reporters began hunting for private
clues, trying to fasten the murders on Heirens and
recorded their progress on page 1.

For more than a month, while Heirens insisted that he
was innocent, Chicago journalism relived Ben Hecht's
and Charles MacArthur's *Front Page*.

The *Hearst Herald-American* started off by importing a
mystery story writer, Craig Rice, from her Santa Monica
home to write about it, and brought the artist, Burris
Jenkins, Jr., from New York to illustrate her articles.
After interviewing the suspect in jail, Mrs. Rice decided
he was innocent, and she wrote: "He's the kind of boy
you could trust your teenage daughter with. I keep
wanting to call him Bill." With its three rivals screaming
"Murder!" the *Herald-American* dropped Craig Rice like a
hot potato.

The papers printed every morsel of information they
could learn about the boy hounded his parents and told
in detail how the three victims had been murdered,
how the little girl was strangled, dismembered with a
knife and her body disposed of in Chicago sewers.

Heirens college room was ransacked, his notes and
books were gone over by reporters.

...

Justice and circulation

By the middle of July, the newspapers began reporting
that Heirens had confessed. The State Attorney's office
and Heirens' counsel denied it. But the papers went
ahead with the stories just the same. The result was

utter confusion to the reader, but—the story sold papers. Marshall Field's *Chicago Sun* jumped thirty thousand in circulation in one day.

The *Chicago Tribune* rocked its competitors by scoring a beat on an alleged confession, with a front-page streamer head, *HOW HEIRENS SLEW 3*. The *Sun* hit the streets at the same time with a contradictory streamer: HEIRENS: NO CONFESSION. But the *Tribune* story forced the *Sun* to reverse itself in later editions with the eight-column headline, HEIRENS CONFESSION. When Heirens finally confessed to the three murders in August, the *Sun* outdid the *Tribune* by running the confession in full—twenty-two columns.

The *Tribune*, trying to live up to its slogan of being "the world's greatest newspaper," claimed four "great beats" during the case. In a three-column story, the *Tribune* wrote:

"For the first time in newspaper history, the detailed story of how three murders were committed, naming the man who did them, was told before the murderer had confessed or was indicted...So great was public confidence in the *Tribune* that other Chicago papers reprinted the story solely because the *Tribune* said it was so. Never has a newspaper's contemporaries, and competitors paid a higher tribute to its reputation for veracity... For a while, Heirens maintained his innocence, but the world believed his guilt. The *Tribune* had said he was guilty."

The Harvard team of Nine Nieman Fellows, experienced reporters/ scholars all, ended their chapter's condemnation of the Heirens coverage by quoting journalists who covered the Heirens story from abroad.

The *Tribune* could boast about "beats" perhaps without regard to its responsibility as a newspaper in giving a man a fair chance. But the British press was shocked at this type of journalism. *The London Sunday Pictorial* attacked the handling of the Heirens case under a five-column headline:

"CONDEMNED BEFORE HIS TRIAL—AMERICA
CALLS THIS JUSTICE."

Writing of the case a week before the confession, the London paper said: "A seventeen-year-old student held by police for questioning has been tried and found guilty of three murders—in the columns of Chicago newspapers. Yet he has not even been charged. It will be hard to pick a jury which has not already read that he is a guilty man.... The whole trial by the press has been carried through while Heirens—as yet innocent in the eyes of all civilized people—is merely held for questioning."

Nieman Fellows, Class of 1946 authors of your Newspaper:
Blueprints for a Better Press *(MacMillan Co. 1947)*

1st row: Ben Yablonky, Robert Manning, Mary Ellen Leary, Cary Robertson, James Batal, Louis Lyons (Curator), Charlotte FitzHenry, Professor Arthur M. Schlesinger Sr.
2nd row: Arthur Hepner, Leon Svirsky, Richard Stockwell, Frank Hewlett.

Inarguably, Heirens's was convicted in a sham Trial by Press. Front-page-style reporters presented sensational and manufactured "evidence" to a lynch mob readership who demanded blood and revenge for the three "Ripper-like" horror murders.

All four Chicago newspapers followed the *Trib*'s lead and placed the completely fabricated "twenty-two-column confession" on the *Trib*'s 'Page One', detailing how Heirens supposedly committed his "Lipstick Murders".

No fact checking on this one. Too big a story, they all just closed their eyes and nodded their heads, Yes, the confession came from an "official and reliable source."
The faux confession was good enough for the public.
 No need for a real trial.

***

Given a choice to live or die, the teenager chose to live, and a month after the newspapers' imaginary confession, which was above the fold nationwide along with a full "Jekyll and Hyde" photo spread of Heirens in *LIFE Magazine*, Bill was forced to "cop a plea."
Never mind that:
1. Heirens passed a lie detector test that showed he was telling the truth that he was innocent and not involved in any of the three murders.
2. The bisection of the Degnan girl was performed by a skilled surgeon and was a delicate and complicated medical procedure known as a "hemicorpectomy."
3. Heirens during his "confession" when asked how he did it informed his interrogators that he "used a hunting knife and did it in the dark in the basement, then threw the knife away." Based on the skill required, which the Degnan Coroner indicated was "beyond his own capabilities," this would have been a physical

impossibility. (This was the exact same surgical bisection operation performed on Elizabeth Short less than a year later in Los Angeles.)

4. Witnesses to the crimes say the suspect was twice Heirens' age and a "tall thin man."

5. The fingerprints claimed to be found at two of the crimes scenes that the police claimed were Heirens' only appeared six months after the crimes and only after his arrest in June 1946. And they were "rolled fingerprints" never found at crime scenes and were only a type obtained during police booking procedures.

6. Heirens in his formal "confession" was unable to give any details of his crimes and for the most part could only say "yes" or "no" to police interrogators and was unaware of how many shots were fired at his victims. (Forced to guess, he claimed "one," but Frances Brown was shot twice.)

No preliminary hearing. No grand jury indictment. No trial. No witness testimony. No evidence offered forth. He was brought before the Court, pled guilty on the condition that he would receive "Life with Parole and not be executed," and was speedily sent to prison. "Case Closed."

William Heirens died in prison on March 5, 2012, while serving his sixty-fifth year for crimes HE DID NOT COMMIT.

Imagine being locked in a six-by-six-foot cell and waking up every day knowing you *are* innocent and counting as the clock ticks off the days, the months, and the years of your life.

Bill Heirens did just that. He counted each day until the clock and his heart stopped on the 23,979th day of his imprisonment.

My heartfelt thanks and utmost respect to all of you who brought a little hope and light into Bill's life.

Especially to Dolores Kennedy his best and closest friend. Dolores never gave up and fought the good fight on behalf of Bill until the very end.

7] Elizabeth Short "The Black Dahlia"-LWM "By Rope, By Knife"

January 15, 1947, Los Angeles, California
(Los Angeles Police Dept)
"The Black Dahlia Murder"

The victim, at age nineteen, left her home in Medford, Massachusetts and came to California.
It is believed she originally met Dr. George Hill Hodel in 1943, as a patient at his First Street VD Clinic in downtown Los Angeles. She was treated by him for a "Bartholin Gland infection," a sexually transmitted disease.

Short is introduced to Hodel's surrealist artist friend and photographer, Man Ray and poses for an oil painting, *L'Equivoque* in 1943. Dr. Hodel becomes "a suitor" and dates, wines, and dines Short on her occasional visits to Hollywood while she is working at the military base at Camp Cook in the Post Exchange as a sales clerk. Short is arrested in 1943 in Santa Barbara for "minor possession" for being present underage in a bar and is sent home to her mother in Medford, Massachusetts.

Based on information contained in the secret DA Hodel/Black Dahlia Files we learn that Short traveled to Chicago, Illinois in June 1946 and began making inquiries into the three "Lipstick Murders." Police reports indicate she became intimate with four separate newspaper reporters and informed them that "she was personally acquainted with a police officer that was working on the Degnan/Heirens case."

Short visits Los Angeles in the summer/fall of 1944 and again in the summer of 1945 and is photographed on VJ Day riding in an open convertible with five other women.

In the fall of 1946, Short returns to Los Angeles and resides at various apartment houses in the Hollywood area. In November 1946, she became fearful for her life and fled to San Diego where she hid out at a private residence for approximately six weeks.

In late December or early January 1947, Short was seen and identified as being in the company of Dr. George Hodel. Both were standing in line waiting to attend a Jack Carson radio show at the CBS Columbia Square Radio Playhouse in Hollywood. On that occasion, George Hodel approached the head usher, Jack Egger, who would later become a prominent witness in the investigation. George produced a police badge identifying himself as "a Chicago police officer" and the usher allowed both Short and Hodel to jump the line (a common courtesy shown to law enforcement) and escorted them to Studio A to see the show.

On January 9, 1947, Elizabeth Short permanently returns from San Diego and is dropped off at the *Biltmore Hotel* by an acquaintance.

During the following week, on separate days and nights, she is seen by more than a dozen witnesses at locations in Hollywood and in the downtown section of LA.

The victim was last seen on the afternoon of January 14, 1947, near the intersection of Fifth and Main Street, in downtown LA, where she spoke with Officer Meryl McBride, an LAPD uniformed policewoman working her beat.

Officer McBride described Short as being both "excited and fearful" as she ran up and informed the officer that "a former suitor was inside a bar down the street and he just threatened to kill me."

Officer McBride accompanied Short back to the bar and recovered the victim's purse, but the man was gone. Officer McBride returned to her foot beat.

An hour later, McBride observed Short a second time exiting a different bar. This time she was in the company of "two men and a woman." McBride approached her and asked, "Are you all right?"

Short replied she was and that she was going to the Greyhound Bus Station down the street to meet her father who was coming into town.

McBride again returned to her duties and this was the last known live sighting of the victim.

The following morning, January 15, 1947, Elizabeth Short's body was found carefully posed on a vacant lot in the Liemert Park section of Los Angeles, some six miles south of Hollywood.

She had been sadistically tortured for hours. Ligature marks were found on her hands, ankles and around her neck, indicating she had been tied then sexually assaulted and anally raped. She had also been force-fed feces. Numerous cuttings were performed on the body and her right breast was removed. (Possibly retained as a "trophy.")

Antemortem, during the torture, the suspect used a cigarette or cigar to inflict 9 separate burn marks to Elsizabeth Short's back.

A "hemicorpectomy" surgical operation, identical to that of victim Suzanne Degnan, had been performed. Her body was posed in the *Minotaur* position (hands bent at the elbows and placed over her head) on a street named "Degnan." (George Hodel thought he was on Degnan, but unbeknownst to him the street changed names mid-block.)

Physical evidence (large paper cement sacks) used to transport the body parts from the original crime scene to the vacant lot would later be connected by this investigator establishing Short had been slain at Dr. George Hodel's Hollywood residence, 5121 Franklin Avenue.

Secret DA Hodel/Black Dahlia Files discovered in 2003 would establish that Dr. George Hill Hodel was her killer, and that electronic surveillance recordings were made containing his confession to this crime as well as other murders and criminal activity.

8] JEANNE AXFORD FRENCH—LWM
"By Knife"

February 10, 1947, Los Angeles, California
(Los Angeles Police Department)
"The Red Lipstick Murder"
aka "Jeanne French: The Flying Nurse Murder"

The victim, age forty, was married, and was last seen dining at a restaurant in West Los Angeles, with a man closely fitting the description of George Hodel. At dinner, the waitress who served them later indicated they were "speaking French." (GHH spoke French fluently.) A male employee observed the couple exit the restaurant and enter the suspect's vehicle, which he described as a 1937 black sedan identical in description to the 1937 black Packard owned and driven by Dr. Hodel.

The killer drove the victim to an isolated vacant lot in the 3200 block of Grandview Ave where he stripped her naked, beat her with what LAPD Police Captain Donahoe described as "a heavy weapon, probably a tire iron or a wrench, as she crouched naked on the highway."

The victim's nude body was dragged from the street to a dirt lot where she was literally stomped to death. The coroner's physician, Dr. Newbarr, found the cause of death to be "ribs shattered by heavy blows, one of the broken ribs having pierced the heart creating hemorrhage and death."

As part of his "posing," the suspect ceremoniously draped the victim's blue coat trimmed with red fox-fur cuffs and her red dress over her nude body. A man's white handkerchief was also found lying nearby. Police recovered black hair follicles from under the victim's fingernails, indicating a violent struggle had occurred prior to her demise.

In a final taunt to the police, as well as to identify himself as "The Black Dahlia Avenger," the same man who tortured and slew Elizabeth Short and posed her body on a vacant lot just three weeks earlier, removed a red lipstick stub from the victim's purse, and wrote a message in large red letters across her nude body. It read: "Fuck You BD."

Top of the next page: Jeanne French's nude body at crime scene.

Bottom photo: Close-up of "Red Lipstick" message written on victim's body, taken at LA Cornoner's office.

9] LAURA ELIZABETH TRELSTAD—LWM "By Rope"

May 11, 1947, Long Beach, California

(Long Beach Police Dept)

"George [Hodel] drowned himself at times in an ocean of deep dreams. Only part of him seemed present. *He would muse standing before one, in a black flowered dressing gown lined with scarlet silk*, [emphasis mine] oblivious to one's presence."
—*Newspaper article, "The Clouded Past of a Poet"*
describing a young George Hodel
by Ted Le Berthon,
Los Angeles Evening Herald, *December 9, 1925*

The victim was a thirty-seven-year-old married mother of three children who had left a party after arguing with her husband.

Mrs. Trelstad went to a Long Beach bar where she continued drinking, and engaged fellow patrons in an argument whereupon the bartender refused to serve her any further drinks. A sailor who had been drinking with her put her on a homeward-bound bus.

Police located the bus driver who recalled the victim being aboard his bus on May 10, 1947. He recalled her due to an incident in which she began arguing with him for passing her stop at Thirty-Sixth Street and American Avenue. She exited the bus at approximately 11:30 p.m. The bus driver recalled seeing a "tall, well-dressed man" follow her off the bus.

On May 11, 1947, at 5:00 a.m., the victim's body was found by an oil field pumper arriving at work at the Signal Hill Oil fields, in Long Beach.

The victim had been severely beaten about the face

and body, raped, and then strangled *"with a piece of flowered cotton cloth, believed torn from a man's pajamas or shorts." [emphasis mine]*

LA County Coroner, Dr. Newbarr, found the cause of death to be "asphyxia due to strangulation, and a skull fracture and hemorrhage and contusion of the brain."

Police detectives at 1947 body dump location of Laura Trelstad near Signal Hills Oil Fields

Police informed the press that "the victim had been murdered elsewhere and the body then dumped in the vacant lot close to the oil rigs." Vehicle tire tracks and footprints were found near the body. Police obtained plaster castings of the footprints.

The fact that the coroner's office affirmed that victim was raped suggests that slides of sperm cells were obtained during the autopsy. If this is confirmed and they still exist, a strong possibility exists that DNA could be obtained and compared to the full DNA profile of George Hodel currently in my possession.

10] MARIAN DAVIDSON NEWTON

The victim's body was discovered by a couple on a hike in the Torrey Pines Mesa area just north of San Diego.

MARIAN DAVIDSON NEWTON—LWM "By Rope"

July 16, 1947, San Diego, California
(San Diego Police Dept)

The victim was an attractive thirty-six-year-old divorcée

vacationing in San Diego from her home in Vancouver, British Columbia.

This crime was identical in nearly all respects to the first Lone Woman Murder of Mrs. Ora Murray that occurred in 1943.

Ms. Newton, accompanied by a female acquaintance, Edna Mitchell, whom she had met at her hotel, decided to go to Sherman's, a popular nightclub /dance hall. A local San Diego attraction that "sported nine different bars and the largest indoor dance floors in the world."

Witness Mitchell would later describe the possible suspect to police as a man who kept dancing with Marian and who was later seen accompanying her from the club. Mitchell described him as "tall, over six foot, thin, possibly in his thirties, with dark hair, wearing a tan sport coat, slacks and a bright-colored tie." The witness earlier in the evening informed the victim that she didn't like the look of the guy and warned her "not to get into a car with any man she met at the club."

On scene, homicide detectives determined that Marian Newton had been strangled with a thin wire or cord.

She suffered blunt force trauma to the body, heavy bruising and had been raped.

Two men's handkerchiefs were found near the body. One was stained and one was not.

The victim's purse and identification had been thrown from the suspect's vehicle and were found in downtown San Diego at the intersection of University and Albatross Streets.

San Diego detectives believed there may have been a connection to this crime and the wave of Lone Woman Murders in Los Angeles and met with LAPD who, despite the strikingly similar MO, expressed doubt to this "outside agency" that the crimes were connected.

11] LILLIAN DOMINGUEZ—LWM
"By Knife"
October 2, 1947, Santa Monica, California
(Santa Monica Police Dept)

This LWM crime was not discovered by me until 2009 and was first summarized in Chapter 11 of *BDA II*, "The Black Dahlia's Three Greatest Myths—Myth No. 1—A Standalone Murder."

The victim, age fifteen, was a student at John Adams Junior High, in Santa Monica, California. She was walking home from a school dance with her sister and a friend.

At the intersection of Seventeenth Street and Michigan, a man approached them and as he walked past he stabbed the victim in the heart with a long thin stiletto-type knife and kept walking.

Lillian yelled out to her friends, "That man just touched me." She took a few more steps and blurted out, "I can't see," then collapsed to the ground and died.

The suspect was only seen from the back as he walked by, so no accurate physical description was ever obtained.

One week to the day of Lillian's murder, her killer left a taunting note that read:

"I killed that Santa Monica girl. I will kill others."

(Note written in pencil & left by killer of Santa Monica teenager, Lillian Dominguez)

Avenger Note Above:

On the evening of October 9, 1947, exactly one-week after the stabbing, Lillian's killer left a handwritten note under the door of a Los Angeles furniture store.

The note was written in pencil on the back of a business card of a Mexican restaurant. (see author reproduction above). While neither the furniture store nor the Mexican restaurant locations were identified by police, the information and threat from the killer was published in the *Santa Monica Evening Outlook* on October 10, 1947, which was George Hodel's fortieth birthday.

We do know that the furniture store was outside the city of Santa Monica and in Los Angeles. We recalled in some of the other Lone Woman murders George Hodel left or mailed the Kern and Short notes just blocks away from his downtown medical office. Was either the furniture store or the Mexican restaurant also near his medical office?

Lillian Dominguez Murder   Santa Monica   October 2, 1947

Los Angeles Times October 3, 1947

Motive Sought in Fatal Knifing of Schoolgirl

Although they continue to interview possible suspects, Santa Monica detectives late yesterday admitted they still are baffled by the mysterious fatal stabbing of Lillian Dominguez, 15-year-old Santa Monica schoolgirl, on her way home from a school dance Wednesday night.

Walking with two other girls, Lillian was approached by a man at 17th St. and Michigan Ave., Santa Monica, at 10 p.m. A moment later, she reeled against a fence saying, "That man touched me. I can't see." A short time later she was pronounced dead on arrival at the Santa Monica Hospital.

Autopsy Performed

Dr. Frederick Newbarr, county autopsy surgeon, reported after performing an autopsy that the stab wound in the girl's left breast is 3½ inches deep and a half inch wide and that it penetrated only the heart muscle, not the heart itself. Death, he said, apparently was caused by internal bleeding. Severance of nerves could have numbed pain and caused the blindness of which the girl complained, Dr. Newbarr said.

Det. Lt. Earl Reinfold of Santa Monica expressed belief that the stabbing could have been done by a sadist or a "hopped up" narcotic addict. No motive for the slaying could be found as Lillian had no boy friends and had no trouble at the dance at the Garfield Elementary School, Santa Monica.

The daughter of Mrs. Emma Dominguez, 1013 17th St., Santa Monica, Lillian was a student at John Adams Junior High School. The girls with her when she was stabbed were her sister, Angie Dominguez, 17, and Andrea Marquez, 17, of 1840 17th St., Santa Monica.

Young California Girl Stabbed by a Man

SANTA MONICA, Calif. (AP)—Lillian Dominguez, a 16-year-old Junior high school girl, was fatally stabbed by an unidentified assailant as she was walking home from a dance last night with two other girls, Police Sgt. J. E. Henry reported.

Police said the girl's companions, Angie Dominguez, 17, her sister, and Andrea Marquez, 17, related that a man approached them from across the street. They said they heard Lillian, who was walking behind them, say, "That man touched me." The two girls said she reeled against a fence and said "I can't see."

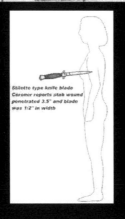

Stiletto type knife blade
Coroner reports stab wound
penetrated 3.5" and blade
was 1/2" in width

12] GLADYS EUGENIA KERN—LWM
"By Knife"
February 14, 1948, Los Angeles
(Los Angeles Police Department)
"The Real Estater Murder"

This victim was a fifty-year-old married woman employed as a real estate agent. Her office was located in the Los Feliz district of Los Angeles (one mile from the home of Dr. George Hill Hodel).

Victim's killer, posing as a home buyer, accompanied her to a vacant private estate in the Hollywood Hills where he and possibly a second man attacked her with an "eight-inch jungle knife" which was left at the scene (found in the kitchen sink, wrapped in a man's handkerchief).

Cause of death was found to be "multiple stab wounds to the body."

On the afternoon of the murder, a Japanese gardener working near the "For Sale" residence observed, "two men walk out of the house and down the steps."
Later descriptions from witnesses who had seen the suspect with Mrs. Kern prior to going to the residence described him as "tall, well dressed, wearing a business suit."

An LAPD police artist obtained a composite drawing, which was published on the front page of the local newspapers.

For comparison purposes I have placed the police composite of the Kern killer in between photos of Dr. George Hill Hodel. No mustache was recalled by witnesses, thus I have intentionally 'airbrushed' it out to show how Hodel would have appeared in the late 1940s and early 50s.

GHH w/o mustache   Police Composite   GHH w/o mustache

The day following the murder, Kern's killer left a long rambling note in a mailbox at Fifth and Olive Streets, revealing the murder.

The writer, feigning illiteracy, gave a very detailed description of the crime prior to the body being found by police.

The note was found just two blocks from Dr. Hodel's medical office and *was posted in the same mailbox in which the Black Dahlia Avenger had left a Dahlia-related note to police a year earlier.*

1948 Kern Murder Note left in mailbox
at Fifth and Olive St. downtown LA.

13] LOUISE MARGARET SPRINGER

George Hodel booking photo taken in October, 1949, just three months after Springer murder showing his, "Black, curly hair."

Photo showing "Springer Murder Car" Article reads, "The discovery has touched off the wildest man hunt since the slaying of the Black Dahlia."

LOUISE MARGARET SPRINGER–LWM
"By Rope"

June 13, 1949, Los Angeles
(Los Angeles Police Department)
"The Green Twig Murder"

This twenty-eight-year-old victim was married and the mother of a two-year-old boy. Her husband, Laurence Springer was a hairstylist of wide reputation employed at a salon on Wilshire Boulevard.

Louise, also a hair stylist, worked in a department store at Santa Barbara and Crenshaw just two blocks from where the body of Elizabeth "Black Dahlia" Short was found.

On June 13, 1947 at 9:05 p.m., the victim finished work and was picked up by her husband in the couple's brand-new 1949 green Studebaker convertible.

Louise discovered she had left her eyeglasses inside and her husband volunteered to go get them, as he also needed to pick up; some ciagrettes in the tobacco store adjacent to the beauty salon. He was absent for only ten minutes.

On his return, he found his wife and their vehicle had disappeared.

After frantically searching the parking lot, he phoned LAPD, who responded, searched the immediate area, and took a "missing report" assuring him that his wife would "likely return in a day or two."

Three days later, the abandoned convertible was found

near downtown Los Angeles. The victim's body was found in the back seat, covered with a beautician's tarp. The cause of death was found to be by "ligature strangulation" with a white precut clothesline cord tied tightly around her neck, which police speculated her killer had brought with him.

Robbery was not a motive as her purse, jewelry, and money were found in the car.

The second shocking discovery appeared in an article in the *Los Angeles Examiner* of June 17, which read:

...

BODY VIOLATED

And with a fourteen-inch length of a finger-thick tree branch, ripped from some small tree, the killer had violated her body in such a manner as to stamp this crime at once and indelibly in the same category as the killing of Elizabeth Short, "the Black Dahlia."

Neighborhood witnesses looking out their window observed a "tall, thin man with black curly hair" exit the Kern vehicle on the night of the kidnapping and walk away. The parked "abandoned" vehicle was not reported to police for several days.

Nota bene:

I have upgraded this crime from its original "Category II" (Probable) in *BDA* (Arcade 2003) to "Category I" (Definite) due to additional information and findings as presented in *BDA II* Chapter 11, "The Black Dahlia's Three Greatest Myths: Myth No. 1—A Standalone Murder."

In 2018, dramatic new *hard evidence* (a seventy-year-old three-page handwritten letter found by witness Sandi Nichols in her mother's personal effects) written by a paid LAPD police informant, actually names George Hodel as the killer of both Elizabeth "Black Dahlia" Short and victim Louise Springer.

The informant, W. Glenn Martin was a personal acquaintance of George Hodel (whom he identifies as "GH" and in his letter, "To Be Opened and read-only in case of Death" goes on the explain his connection to "GH" and that both he and "GH"personally were acquainted with victim Springer prior to her murder.

The Martin Letter details "GH's" involvement with corruption and police payoffs and how "GH" was "let go" on the crimes by friendly police detectives. (See full details in the Afterword Chapter of *Black Dahlia Avenger III* (Rare Bird Books 2018).

14] MIMI BOOMHOWER–LWM

(Left) Police and press noted the similarities of the Boomhower crime to the murder of real estate agent Gladys Kern in February 1948 and headlined the connection, "Wealthy Widow Feared Victim of Knife Slayer. Police Recall Still Unsolved Kern Killing."

(Right) Photo of purse left at a phone booth on which is probable suspect(s) handprinted message to police.

See page 200 "Additional Photos" for enhanced view of the writing on the Boomhower purse.

MIMI BOOMHOWER–LWM
(Unknown cause of death body not found)

August 18, 1949, Los Angeles
(Los Angeles Police Department)
"The Merry Widow Murder"

The victim Mimi Boomhower was a Bel-Air socialite and "prominent heiress," age forty-eight.

Mrs. Boomhower was last heard from on August 18, 1949, when she spoke with her business manager and informed him "she was meeting a gentleman at 7:00 p.m. at her home" whom the manager believed was a prospective buyer for the mansion.

Police surmised the victim was abducted from her home with a possible motive of robbery, though numerous items of value had been left inside her private residence.

Mimi Boomhower was never heard from or seen again nor was her body ever found.
The possible suspect(s) left her purse just a few miles from her hillside mansion at a phone booth in Beverly Hills.

The following message to the police was written in large printed letters on the Boomhower purse:

```
POLICE DEPT.—
WE FOUND THIS
  AT BEACH
THURSDAY NIGHT
```

Handwriting analysis of the letters on the purse was conducted by court-certified Questioned Document Expert, Hannah McFarland.

Her comparison to known samples of the hand-printing of Dr. George Hill Hodel resulted in a finding that it was "highly probable that he wrote the message to police."

(QDE McFarland also analyzed and found that the lipstick hand-printing on the body of Mrs. Jeanne French was "highly probably written by Dr. George Hodel.")

15] JEAN ELIZABETH SPANGLER–LWM (Unknown cause of death, body not found)

October 7, 1949, Hollywood, California
(Los Angeles Police Department)

The victim was a twenty-seven-year-old Hollywood actress who had been a former dancer at Black Dahlia witness Mark Hansen's Florentine Gardens nightclub. She was recently divorced and living with her five-year-old-daughter Christine in an apartment in Hollywood. Tracing her movements on the evening of October 7 until she was last seen in the early morning hours of October 8, 1949, police determined the following:

The victim was seen with a handsome dapper-dressed male sitting in his dark-colored sedan parked in the Hollywood Ranch Market lot. (The descriptions fit both George Hodel and his vehicle, a 1937 black Packard. The location was just seventy-five feet from his good friend Man Ray's residence apartment at the Villa Elaine, 1245 N. Vine St. It should be further noted that George Hodel was released from jail on the incest/child molestation charges on the previous morning, October 6, after posting cash bail.)

On the early morning hours of October 8, the victim was seen seated with two men at a front row table at the Cheese Box Restaurant, 8033 Sunset Boulevard.

They were having an argument and as the restaurant's radio personality "Al the Sheik" Lazaar approached the actress for a live interview, the man, fitting Dr. Hodel's description, brusquely signaled to him "no interview" and Lazaar veered away. (As to the public argument, I find myself asking, "Could it be related to the fact that GHH had been arrested the day previous and charged with having sexual relations with Tamar, his fourteen-year-old daughter?)

The last sighting of the victim was by a gas station attendant at a service station just a few blocks from the restaurant, shortly after the argument.

The driver pulled his car to the gas pumps and had the attendant fill the tank, saying, "We're going to Fresno." Jean Spangler shrank down in the front seat, and as the car pulled away, she yelled to the witness, "Have the police follow this car." The attendant immediately called LAPD who responded but were unable to locate the vehicle or Jean Spangler.

Black Dahlia Avenger III [page 195]

Jean's sister-in-law, Sophie Spangler, who was babysitting Jean's daughter, Christine, phoned the police and made a formal "Missing Report" on Saturday, October 8 at 9:00 a.m.

Spangler's purse was found twenty-four hours later on Sunday at 11:00 a.m., discarded off the roadway in Fern Dell Park, a short distance from the Hodel residence.

Like the previous victim, Mimi Boomhower, Jean Spangler's body was never found, and the exact cause of death remains unknown.

Spangler's divorce attorney, S.S. Hahn (who was also the attorney who represented my mother, Dorothy Hodel in her 1945 divorce from George Hodel) shortly after the disappearance of his client publicly announced, "foul play is suspected."

WEATHER
Clear and continued mild to-day and Thursday. Patches of fog late tonight.

Long Beach Independent

Long Beach 12, Calif., Wednesday Morning, Oct. 12, 1949

HOME EDITION

5c

TV ACTRESS FEARED VICTIM OF SEX FIEND

Ex-Wilton Owner In Control

Long Beach's largest motel—the Wilton—changed ownership Tuesday when Frank Fishman, former owner, on a revolution of current equity remained direction and ownership of the motel property at 416 E. Ocean blvd.

The Wilton, which Fishman bought two years ago from Floyd Hilton for a reported $2 million, was sold to the Wilton several months ago.

Fishman, former hotel operator, refused to say anything further in the hotel when asked Tuesday.

On Sept. 26 Fishman filed a suit in superior court demanding that a receiver be appointed for the hotel and that Hilton be forced to account for hotel assets.

The suits Fishman said, would tie it and he pledged himself to do all in my power to make the Wilton the best hotel on the Pacific Coast.

Atty. Robert Light, Los Angeles, represented Fishman, and Atty. Henry Miller, Los Angeles, represented Hilton.

Fishman, who comes here builds throughout the country and tells dispute after the agreement.

Acheson to Testify
WASHINGTON — (UP) Secretary of State Acheson is scheduled to testify at a closed session of the Senate Foreign Relations committee today with clarification concerning our policy around China policy.

Council Sets Date For Rent Showdown

What may be the final round in the verbal battle over local rent regulation will be fought at 7:30 p.m. Oct. 26 in council chambers.

This was place of the second public hearing on the controversial measure vote was set Tuesday by the city council. The council by the city council.

'Meanest Thief' Caught by Newsboy
Jimmie J. Sinks, of the blocks old, 12-year-old newsboy who apprehends a thief at Birch st. and Pine ave. caught a "meanest thief" in the act Tuesday, police reported.

He detected a juvenile taking a paper from the curb and "billing" the contents of depositing a coin.

Jimmie chased the suspect, who retrieved the paper, collared at 3 cents.

Public Offices, Banks Closed Today
Banks and public offices will be shut down today in recognition of the fact that Columbus sighted America Oct. 12, 1492.

Columbus was presented, supposedly, pay, by Scandinavian explorers, but there's always give the credit. Who, for example, ever heard of Leif Ericsson Day?

City Survey Demanded
The Tenant's Civic Council, in a letter signed by A. V. Aldrich, secretary, distributed the city's personnel.

Air Training Transfer Asked
The city's formal request for transfer of the air force training activities from the local training stations here has been submitted to W. S. Symington, secretary of the air force.

This was reported in the city council today in a letter from C. J. Brown, administrative secretary to Louis Johnson, secretary of national defense, to whom the request was made.

JEAN SPANGLER . . . latest L. A. Sex Fiend Victim?

(Continued on Page 2)

Hunt Body In L. A. City Park

HOLLYWOOD — (UP). The possibility of another in a long series of fiendish sex murders was feared Los Angeles police today as they prepared to enlarge the mysterious disappearance of Jean Spangler, 27-year-old glamorous actress who had stood around in park since Saturday.

The only clue was her purse, ripped and torn as apparent evidence of a struggle. It was found in the 450 acres of Griffith Park's hilly brush and tangled brush.

Early today an army of 200 volunteers and trusties began a search in the park's Fern Dell ravine, the bottom of the canyon running northwest side of her home.

Her daughter, 5-year-old Christine, Friday also made witch it kiss and told her she was going to meet her father.

ROBERT CUMMINGS Jean Said Was of Romance

One clue, 36, Sophie Spangler, Jean also was "off to work."

The mystery of the actress' whereabouts deepened when police worked through her casting mother who said her last known costume was not—

(Continued on Page 2)

PRETTY BONITA JANE WALTER . . . Not Jean Spangler

Waitress Mistaken For Missing Actress

Four hours or four hours each were not job-hunting when she looked for the missing Jean Spangler—a 25-year-old Long Beach woman Tuesday worked the switchboard, then running to help a Jean Rose. Walter, they she's not missing, and for doesn't even know Jean Spangler.

Bonita, who lives in a motel at Seventh and Elm ave. made several of Jean Spangler's Tuesday afternoon. "I am convinced mistaken, she

(Continued on Page 2)

Mrs. FDR 65
NEW YORK—(UP)—It was Mrs. Franklin D. Roosevelt's 65th birthday today, but she could not devote much time to celebrating. She had to be on call as a United States delegate to the United Nations general assembly session in New York.

Let's Hear It All   **Features Index**

Long Beach Independent October 12, 1949

LAPD officers pointing to where victim Jean Spangler's ripped purse was found in Ferndell Park. More than two hundred officers searched this west side area of Griffith Park on foot and horseback.

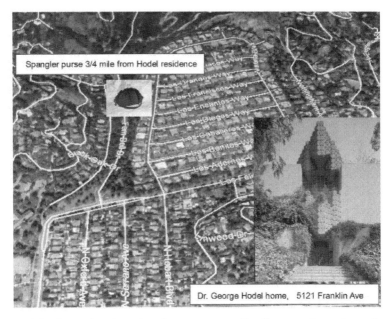

Aerial photo showing the three-quarter-mile distance from Spangler purse to Dr. George Hodel's then private residence at 5121 Franklin Ave.

Jean Spangler's updated findings and linkage to Dr. George Hill Hodel were presented in *BDA II* (2014 ed.), Chapter 24, "Odor Mortis: The Smell of Death—Jean Spangler Background and Last Known Movements."

16] JANE DOE—LWM (Possible drugging and blunt force trauma, body not found)

February 18, 1950, Hollywood, California
(Los Angeles Police Department jurisdiction. No known investigation ever conducted by LAPD. DA detectives initiated a cursory investigation based on electronic surveillance tapes, but the suspected crime was never made public.)

The victim was an unidentified female "Jane Doe" who had gone to the residence of Dr. George Hill Hodel on the afternoon of February 18, 1947.

Unbeknownst to Hodel and others at the residence, the LADA was electronically staked out at the home and recording conversations and activities.

The victim was overhead being offered alcoholic drinks and was possibly drugged.

Dr. Hodel is overheard saying, "Let's have another drink. Does your husband know you're here?"

In the afternoon hours, the victim was recorded crying and attempting to call the telephone operator but dropped the phone and was disconnected. It is believed she was drugged and attempting to call for help.

Hours later, Dr. Hodel and an accomplice, later identified by me as "Baron Ernst Harringa," a longtime Hodel acquaintance and DTLA art gallerist, are recorded going downstairs to the basement.

An object is heard striking what is believed to be the Jane Doe victim. She screams. More blows are overheard, and more screams, then Dr. Hodel is recorded saying to "The Baron," "Don't leave a trace."

Based on these recorded statements and actions, DA Detective McGrath conducted a follow-up investigation and interviewed a plumber who had been summoned to the Hodel residence to "clear a drain in the basement." McGrath inquired if he had "seen any signs of digging in the basement." Witness stated, "He wasn't looking for anything like that and just did his job and left." McGrath made a formal report documenting his investigation.

This female "Jane Doe" victim was never identified and her body, like that of Mimi Boomhower and Jean Spangler, was never found.

The Victims—Part II 1966-1969

17. CHERI JO BATES—ZK "By Knife"

October 30, 1966, Riverside, California (Riverside Police Department)

The victim, age eighteen, was a student at Riverside City College, located approximately eighty miles east of Los Angeles, California.

On the evening of October 30, 1966, after conducting some research at the college library, she exited and walked to her car, a lime-green Volkswagen Bug.

She attempted to start her car, but unbeknownst to her, the suspect had opened the hood and ripped out the distributor cap and coil and wires, making the vehicle inoperable.

As she stood by her car, a male approached and offered her a ride, and she apparently accepted his offer, and as Cheri Jo walked with the man to his car, he turned, viciously attacked her with a knife, and cut her throat, leaving her for dead.

A campus groundskeeper found her body on the ground the following morning.

Riverside Police responded to the crime scene and discovered that the victim had been badly beaten about the face and head, with multiple stab wounds to her chest and back. Her jugular vein had been severed so savagely she was nearly decapitated.

The victim was clutching a tuft of what is believed to be her killer's hair in her right hand.

Robbery was not a motive as her purse and contents were left at the scene. Authorities indicated she was not sexually assaulted.

One month to the day from her murder, the

suspect mailed a lengthy typewritten "confession" to both the Riverside Police Department and the local newspaper.

Sadistic in the extreme, typed in all capital letters, it read:

THE CONFESSION
BY - - - - - - - - - - - -
SHE WAS YOUNG AND BEAUTIFUL. BUT NOW SHE IS BATTERED AND DEAD. SHE IS NOT THE FIRST AND SHE WILL NOT BE THE LAST. I LAY AWAKE NIGHTS THINKING ABOUT MY NEXT VICTIM. MAYBE SHE WILL BE THE BEAUTIFUL BLOND THAT BABYSITS NEAR THE LITTLE STORE AND WALKS DOWN THE DARK ALLEY EACH EVENING ABOUT SEVEN. OR MAYBE SHE WILL BE THE SHAPELY BLUE EYED BROWNETT THAT SAID NO WHEN I ASKED HER FOR A DATE IN HIGH SCHOOL. BUT MAYBE IT WILL NOT BE EITHER. BUT I SHALL CUT OFF HER FEMALE PARTS AND DEPOSIT THEM FOR THE WHOLE CITY TO SEE. SO DON'T MAKI IT TO EASY FOR ME. KEEP YOUR SISTERS, DAUGHTERS, AND WIVES OFF THE STREETS AND ALLEYS. MISS BATES WAS STUPID. SHE WENT TO THE SLAUGHTER LIKE A LAMB. SHE DID NOT PUT UP A STRUGGLE. BUT I DID. IT WAS A BALL. I FIRST PULLED THE MIDDLI WIRE FROM

THE DISTRIBUTOR. THEN I
WAITED FOR HER IN THE LIBRARY
AND FOLLOWED HER OUT AFTER
ABOUT TWO MINUTS. THE BATTERY
MUST HAVE BEEN ABOUT DEAD BY
THEN I THEN OFFERED TO HELP.
SHE WAS THEN VERY WILLING TO
TALK WITH ME. I TOLD HER THAT
MY CAR WAS DOWN THE STREET
AND THAT I WOULD GIVE HER A
LIFT HOME. WHEN WE WERE
AWAY FROM THE LIBRARY
WALKING. I SAID IT WAS BOUT
TIME. SHE ASKED ME, "ABOUT TIME
FOR WHAT". I SAID IT WAS ABOUT
TIME FOR HER TO DIE. I GRABBED
HER AROUND THE NECK WITH MY
HAND OVER HER MOUTH AND
MY OTHER HAND WITH A SMALL
KNIFE AT HER THROAT. SHE WENT
VERY WILLINGLY. HER BREAST
FELT VERY WARM AND FIRM
UNDER MY HANDS. BUT ONLY ONE
THING WAS ON MY MIND. MAKING
HER PAY FOR THE BRUSH OFFS
THAT SHE HAD GIVEN ME DURING
THE YEARS PRIOR. SHE DIED HARD.
SHE SQUIRMED AND SHOOK AS I
CHOAKED HER. AND HER LIPS
TWICHED. SHE LET OUT A
SCREAM OXCE AND I KICKED HER
HEAD TO SHUT HER UP. I PLUNGED
THE KNIFE INTO HER AND IT BROKE.
I THEN FINISHED THE JOB BY
CUTTING HER THROAT. I AM NOT
SICK. I AM INSANE. BUT THAT
WILL NOT STOP THE GAME. THIS

LETTER SHOULD BE PUBLISHED
FOR ALL TO READ IT. IT JUST
MIGHT SAVE THAT GIRL IN THE
ALLEY. BUT THAT'S UP TO YOU. IT
WILL BE ON YOUR CONSCIENCE.
NOT MINE. YES, I DID MAXE THAT
CALL TO YOU ALSO. IT WAS JUST A
WARNING. BEWARE...I AM STALKING
YOUR GIRLS NOW.

CC. CHIEF OF POLICE
ENTERPRISE

This "confession" was followed-up by the killer mailing a six-month anniversary note, on April 30, 1967, written in large block letters which the suspect sent to the police, the press, and to the victim's parents at their home address.

The note read:

BATES
HAD TO
DIE THERE
WILL BE
MORE

Z

A third message, a poem carved into one of the library desks and discovered after the crime, pointed to the likelihood that Cheri's killer had stalked her inside the library, probably lay in wait, and watched her while she conducted her research.

The poem read:

> Sick of living/unwilling to die cut.
> clean.
> if **red**/
> clean.
> blood spurting,
> dripping,
> spilling;
> all **over** her new
> dress
> **oh** well
> **it** was red
> anyway.
> life draining into
> an uncertain
> death. she won't
> **die**.
> this **time**
> someone
> find her.
> just wait till
> next time.
> rh[6]

6 At the time of the murder, R. H. Bradshaw was the president of Riverside City College. Police *speculated* the killer may have known this and possibly used his initials as part of a subtle taunt.

Cheri Jo Bate's killer's three (3) separate 1966-1967 taunting messages.

Upper Left -- is the typed "confession"

Upper Right -- the *"Bates Had To Die; There Will Be More"*

Lower Left -- *is a photograph of the poem written on the desktop inside the library while he stalked his victim immedieatly before the assault and murder.*

Los Angeles Times

ZODIAC LINKED TO RIVERSIDE SLAYING

Pressure Builds
on Californias

Growing Atmo-
Police move to

Notes About
Coed's Death
There Cited

Los Angeles Times, **November 16, 1970**
headline announcing **police link Zodiac Killer to**
Southern California, **Cheri Jo Bates murder**.

18. LUCILA LALU—ZK "By Knife, By Rope"

May 28, 1967, Manila, Philippines (Manila Metropolitan Police Department) "The Jigsaw Murder," aka "The Chop Chop Murder."

"I SHALL CUT OFF HER FEMALE PARTS AND DEPOSIT THEM FOR THE WHOLE CITY TO SEE."

Z (Cheri Jo Bates Confession Letter, Nov. 30, 1966)

"BATES HAD TO DIE THERE WILL BE MORE"

Z (Cheri Jo Bates Note April 30, 1967)

Victim Lucila "Lucy" Lalu y Tolentino was an attractive twenty-nine-year old businesswoman. Lucy owned Lucy's Beauty Salon and The Pagoda Cocktail Bar in the city of Manila, Philippines. Both businesses shared the same address.

Curious crowd gathered in front of Lucy's House of Beauty on Maybaligue st. where Lucila Lalu was murdered. then mutilated on the night of May 28. The house of death is a two-story apartment building.

(Left) Victim, Lucila Lalu y Tolentino (Right) Lucy's House of Beauty. A crowd gathered after hearing about the "Chop Chop Murder."

On the night of May 28, 1967, the victim was assaulted in her place of business. She was beaten about the face and body, and police speculated that she was then forced into a waiting vehicle.

Miss Lalu was taken to an unknown location where after having her hands bound with a rope she was then strangled to death.

Her body was bisected as well as having her arms and legs disarticulated by what the Manila Coroner said, "Had to have been performed by a skilled surgeon."

The victim's upper torso was placed just off the street adjacent to a vacant lot. Her disarticulated lower legs were taken to a separate section of the city where they were wrapped in newspaper and placed atop a trash can.

The victim had been decapitated, and the head was never found.

The victim was initially a "Jane Doe" until her fingerprints were checked and found to be on file in the Manila Police Department from when she had previously filed to be a waitress in a restaurant.

The Manila Times

MANILA, PHILIPPINES, WEDNESDAY, MAY 31, 1967

Girl's headless
body identified

Manila Times announcing body identified from fingerprints.

Map of Manila, Philippines & Makati District
1) George Hodel's Office
2) George Hodel's Family Residence
3) Lalu body found off Zodiac Street

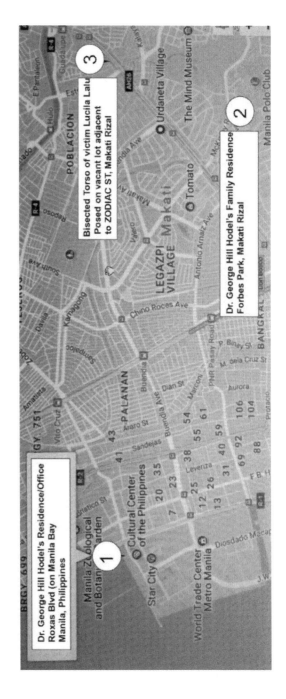

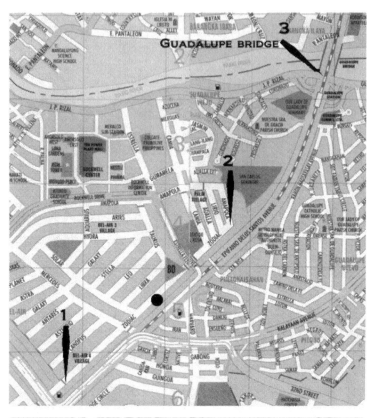

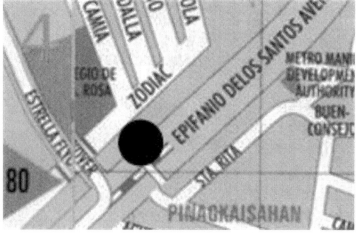

Makati District (enlargement)
shows **body's location** adjacent to **"Zodiac Street."**

19-20. BETTY JENSEN AND DAVID FARADAY—ZK "By Gun" December 20, 1968, Vallejo, California (Solano County Sheriffs)

Victims Betty Lou Jensen, age 16, and David Faraday, age 17, were on their "first date" after attending their Hogan High School Christmas Concert.

Both teenagers were residents of Vallejo, California.

At approximately 11:30 p.m., the young couple drove and parked in an isolated "lovers' lane" location on Herman Road, near the entrance to the Benicia Water Pumping Station.

Shortly after David parked his 1961 Rambler station wagon, a second car pulled up and parked nearby.

The suspect, armed with a .22-caliber semi-automatic handgun, approached the couple and fired a shot through the rear window of the vehicle.

Both victims attempted to exit the right front passenger door. David was shot in the head, and Betty Lou was shot five times in the back as she attempted to flee on foot and collapsed just ten feet to the rear of the vehicle.

Police determined that a total of ten shots were fired.

The cause of death to both victims was found to be "gunshot wounds." A witness came forward who had just driven by the location and heard shots and had observed a second vehicle parked next to the Faraday station wagon, but could not describe the make or model, nor could he provide a suspect description.

The crime remained an isolated, motiveless, apparent random double-homicide with no real leads.

It would not be connected to "The Zodiac Killings" until Zodiac claimed ownership in 1969

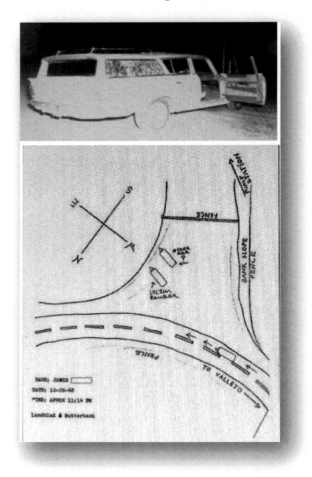

(Top) Photo of Faraday Rambler station wagon at scene
(Bottom) Police sketch of Herman Road and vehicles per
eyewitness description.

4— Santa Cruz Sentinel   Sunday, December 22, 1968

Two Vallejo Teenagers Found Slain On Road

Vallejo (AP) — Investigators quizzed friends of two Vallejo teenagers yesterday searching for clues in their double murder Friday night as they returned from a high school Christmas concert.

Bettilou Jensen, 16, and David Faraday, 17, were found sprawled on the side of a lonely road about 10 miles east of Vallejo, shot in a volley of rifle fire. Investigators described the double slaying as "exceptionally gruesome."

Mrs. Manuel Borges, who was en route to pick up her children at a movie in nearby Benicia, saw the bodies in the headlights of her car and notified police.

Faraday, a senior at Vallejo High School where he was on the wrestling team, died en route to a hospital. Miss Jensen, a junior at Vallejo's Hogan High School, was dead at the scene.

Coroner Dan Horan said investigators were looking into the possibility the young couple, who were on their first date, had been trailed from the concert at Hogan High.

Horan said the youngsters had "apparently just stopped" on the road, a favorite parking spot for young couples, when the shootings occurred. The car's heater was still running when investigators arrived.

They said: Faraday was shot in the left side of the head after getting out of his car and walking around to the passenger side.

Miss Jensen then apparently ran and was shot in the back with five .22-caliber bullets at a range of about 10 feet. Four spent .22-caliber shell casings were found at the scene. There was a bullet hole in the back window of the car.

Investigators described both victims as "good kids from nice homes." They said neither "had ever been in any kind of trouble."

Faraday, son of Mr. and Mrs. Jean L. Faraday, was an Eagle Scout and held the God and Country Award, one of scouting's highest honors. His father works for the Pacific Gas and Electric Co.

Miss Jensen was the daughter of Mr. and Mrs. Vincent M. Jensen. Her father is a programmer for the U.S. General Services Administration.

Santa Visits Fatherless Of Farmington

Farmington, W.Va. (AP).—Santa and Mrs. Claus came to this grief-stricken coal mining community yesterday and for a brief moment the children

21-22. DARLEEN FERRIN AND MICHAEL MAGEAU—ZK "By Gun"

July 4, 1969 Vallejo, California (Vallejo Police Dept.)

Victim Darleen Ferrin, age twenty-two, and Michael Mageau, age nineteen, were seated in Darleen's 1963 Corvair in an isolated parking lot adjacent to Blue Rock Springs Park, in Vallejo, California.

The suspect drove up and parked nearby; then approached the couple on foot holding a flashlight in hand and shined it in Mageau's face.

He then, without saying a word, fired multiple rounds at both victims while they remained seated inside the parked car.

Both victims were found fifteen minutes after the shooting by a passing motorist who summoned the police and ambulance.

Mageau survived his gunshot wounds, but Darleen Ferrin died in the ambulance while en route to the hospital.

Mageau was unable to provide any accurate description of the shooter, informing the police, "He was a white male. It was dark, and I only saw his profile. I never saw his face from the front."

On July 5, shortly after the shooting, the suspect, calling from a payphone just a few blocks from the Vallejo Police Station, called the police department and stated:

> I want to report a double murder. If you
> will go one mile east on Columbus Parkway
> to the public park, you will find the kids in a

brown car. They were shot with a nine-millimeter Luger. I also killed those kids last year. Good-bye.

On July 31, 1969, the killer mailed a two-page handwritten letter to the *San Francisco Chronicle* identifying himself as the shooter in both the Jensen/Faraday and Mageau/Ferrin shootings.

On August 2, the suspect provided more information along with a three-part cryptogram and for the first time would announce himself to the public in what would become his familiar introduction, "This is the Zodiac Speaking..."

Along with providing his new "Zodiac" pseudonym, he would henceforth sign his letters with the familiar cross-and-circle zodiac symbol.

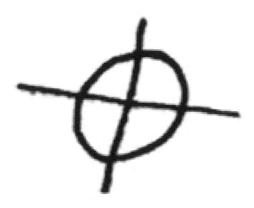

The Zodiac's Signature

Letter mailed to San Francisco Chronicle *July 31, 1969*

Dear Editor

This is the murderer of the
2 teenagers last Christmass
at Lake Herman + the girl
on the 4th of July near
the golf course in Vallejo
To prove I killed them I
Shall state some facts which
only I + the police know.
Christmass
1 Brand name of ammo
  Super X
2 10 shots were fired
3 the boy was on his back
  with his feet to the car.
4 the girl was on her right
  side feet to the west
4th July
1 girl was wearing patterned
  slacks
2 The boy was also shot in
  the knee.
3 Brand name of ammo was
  Western
Over—

Here is part of a cipher the
other 2 parts of this cipher are
being mailed to the editors of
the Vallejo times   + SF Exam
iner.
I want you to print this cipher on the front page of you.
paper. In this cipher is my
identity.
If you do not print this cipher
by the afternoon of Fry. 1st of
Aug 69, I will go on a kill ram-
Page Fry. night. I will cruse
around all weekend killing lone
People in the night then move
on to kill again, untill I end
up with a dozen people over
the weekend.

S. F. Chronicle
San Fran. Calif
Please Rush to
Editor !

Zodiac's three-part cryptogram published August 3, 1969

23-24. CECELIA SHEPARD AND BRYAN HARTNELL—ZK
"By Rope, By Knife, By Gun" ZK
September 27 , 1969 Napa (Napa Sheriff's Department)

Victims Cecelia Shepard, age twenty-two, and her boyfriend, Bryan Hartnell, age twenty, had driven to Lake Berryessa in Bryan's Karmann Ghia to view the sunset.

The young couple was seated on a blanket at shore side when they were approached by a man wearing an "executioner's type hood and tunic." Sewn or drawn on the tunic was a three-inch cross-and-circle, identical to the one the Ferrin/Mageau shooter had been using as his signature in his August 3, 1969 "This is the Zodiac Speaking..." mailings to the press.

The suspect, armed with a large blue-steel automatic handgun, stated to victim Hartnell, "I want your car keys and money. My car is hot... I'm going to Mexico."

Removing some precut lengths of clothesline from his pocket, the assailant told Cecelia to tie up her boyfriend. She followed his instructions. He then ordered Hartnell to get on the ground and further hogtied his hands and feet.

Without warning, the masked man began stabbing both victims with a long bayonet-type knife. Cecelia was stabbed multiple times in both the front and back of her body and Bryan was then stabbed numerous times in the back.

The suspect fled on foot, leaving both victims for dead.

A passing boat motorist heard Bryan's call for help and summoned the police.

Both victims were rushed to the hospital, and while Bryan Hartnell would survive, Cecelia would succumb to her multiple stab wounds two days later.

Hartnell was unable to provide an accurate description of the suspect as he claimed he "only saw him in profile through the eyehole in the mask."

A month later, on October 24, 1969, Hartnell was contacted by a San Francisco Police Department sketch artist and provided the below composite of how "Zodiac" appeared during the Lake Berryessa attack on himself and Cecelia Shepard.

Suspect descriptors provided by Hartnell were notated on the sketch artist's drawing:

"5' 11, Dark hair, clip on sunglasses, black gloves, Blue steel semi-automatic, foot long knife, 1" x 12" wood sheath, boots pants tucked in boot, pleated slacks, 3"x 3" symbol."

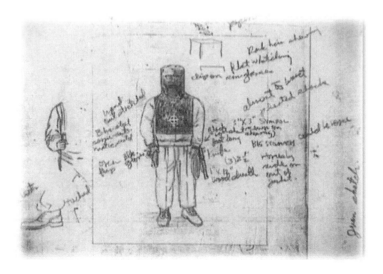

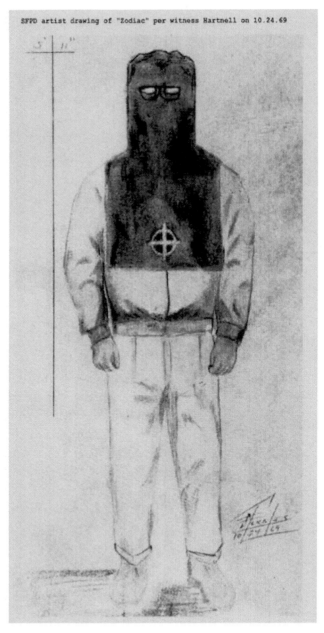

SFPD artist drawing of "Zodiac" per witness Hartnell on 10.24.69

Completed Artist's Rendering of Zodiac

The killer before leaving the crime scene took the time to write the following unique taunt on the passenger door of Bryan's Karmann Ghia, which was parked at the roadside.

Seen here in this crime scene photo:

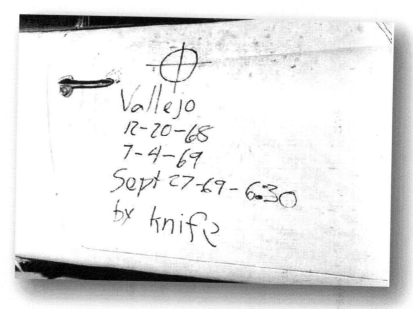

His message was clear. Beginning with his Zodiac signature symbol, he was taking credit for the Jensen/Faraday attack of 12/20/68, the Ferrin/Mageau attack of 7/4/69, and now, today, "By knife" he committed the Shepard/Hartnell attack of 9/27/69.

Vallejo
12-20/68
7-4-69
Sept 27-69 – 6:30
by knife

Furthermore, to underscore his authenticity, Zodiac drove to downtown Napa to a phone booth outside of a car wash, just four blocks from the police station— just as he had done in the Ferrin/Mageau crime.

He then called the police dispatcher and stated:

Caller:
I want to report a murder—no a double murder. They are two miles north of Park Headquarters. They were in a white Volkswagen Karmann Ghia.

Police:
Where are you?

Caller:
I'm the one who did it. (Hangs up phone)

"By Rope"

Red Lipstick Killer

CLEW—This soiled piece of a clothes line is believed to have been used in the gruesome killing of Suzanne. It was found in the basement of building in which Hector Verburgh, the suspect, served as a janitor.

Black Dahlia Avenger

NOOSE—Here is the skillfully knotted and tightly drawn rope with which Mrs. Louise Springer was strangled by fiend. —Los Angeles Examiner photo.

Manila Jigsaw Killer

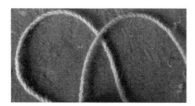

Zodiac

(Photo Lower Right) Napa Sheriff's evidence photograph showing precut clothesline used by "Zodiac" to bind victims Hartnell & Shepard at Lake Berryessa.

Bringing precut clothesline to a crime is a highly unusal "MO"; however, we know George hodel did so in Chicago Lipstick Murder (Photo Upper Left); in the Manila Jigsaw Murder* (Photo Lower Left); and (Photo Upper Right) in the Black Dahlia Avenger/LA Lone Woman Murders. *Author reproduced image.

25. PAUL STINE—ZK "By Gun"
October 11, 1969 San Franscico, CA, San Francisco P.D.)

Victim Paul Stine was a 29-year-old graduate student at San Francisco State College who was driving part-time for Yellow Cab Company.

On the evening of October 11, 1969, the victim, driving his Yellow Cab taxi, was hailed by a male near Powell and Geary Streets in downtown San Francisco.

His passenger (the suspect) instructed him to drive to "Washington and Maple" in Presidio Heights.

As the cab approached its destination, Stine was told to drive one more block, to the intersection of Washington and Cherry.

Without warning, the suspect then placed a 9mm handgun to the victim's right temple and fired one round, execution-style.

Teenagers heard the shot from their upstairs bedrrom across the street and looked out their window in time to observe the suspect standing at the open right front passenger door of the Yellow Cab.

The shooter appeared to be rifling his clothes and robbing the cab driver, whose body was slumped over in the front seat.

(It was later determined that the suspect was rippig or cutting a section of the victim's bloodied shirt which the suspect took with him.)

The teens immediately telephoned the police and continued to watch as the man removed a white rag or handkerchief from his pocket and began wiping down the exterior doors on both the passenger and driver's side of the cab.

San Francisco: Paul Stine cab at Zodiac crime scene
Washington and Cherry Streets on October 11, 1969

(Left) *Stine's bloody shirt and men's leather gloves size 7 booked as evidence by SFPD.* (Right) *George & June Hodel (circa 1995) Orcas Island, Washington. GHH seen putting on his leather gloves (believed to be "size 7") a regular part of his accoutrement.*

The teens watched as the shooter walked northbound on Cherry Street, out of sight.

The following description was immediately provided to SFPD uniformed officers from the four witnesses:

"Male, White, early forties, 5-8, crewcut hair, dark glasses, wearing dark brown trousers, dark shoes and dark blue or black parka jacket."

During the assault, the suspect left a pair of men's gloves, size 7, inside the Stine taxi, which were blood splattered and booked into evidence.

A responding patrol unit observed a male Caucasian walking down the street just a few blocks away whom they questioned and released.

Two days after the shooting, "**Zodiac**" sent another taunting **letter** to the press and police **taking credit for** the **Stine murder and included a piece of the victim's torn bloody shirt as proof**.

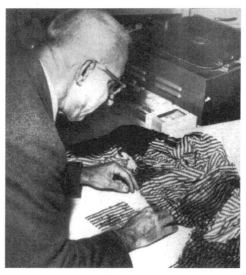

SFPD Criminalist compares the bloody section of shirt (mailed to the press by Zodiac) to the bloody shirt booked as evidence in the Stine murder.

Almost one month later, on November 9, 1969, "Zodiac" sent a second lengthy six-page letter to his favorite newspaper of choice, *The San Francisco Chronicle*. (George Hodel was employed as a reporter/columnist for that newspaper in the 1930s.)

In addition to a detailed description of his various crimes in a highlighted "P.S. Must Print in paper," Zodiac "called out" the uniformed officers who responded to the Stine shooting. Zodiac informed the public that the two officers stopped and talked to him, and he sent them off on a ruse telling them he "saw a man running down the street with a gun in his hand" at which point they took off in fresh pursuit, allowing him to escape into the night.

Here is the "P.S." portion of the letter mailed to the *San Francisco Chronicle* which, at Zodiac's insistence, the newspaper published three days later, on Nov. 12, 1969.

It read:

Ps. 2 cops pulled a goof abot 3 min after I left the cab.
I was walking down the hill to the park when this cop car pulled up & one of them called me over & asked if I saw any one acting supicisous [sic] Or strange in the last 5 to 10 min & I said yes there was this man who was Running by waveing [sic] a gun & the cops peeled rubber & went around the corner as I directed them & I disappeared into the park a block & a half away never to be seen again. Hey pig doesn't it rile you up to have your noze rubed [sic] in your booboos?

Zodiac – November 9, 1969 Letter – (page 3)
Printed in newspaper on November 12, 1969

The publication of Zodiac's ridiculing of SFPD patrol officers for "Question and Releasing" him and mocking them for their "booboos" forced the involved Officer Fouke to write a responding internal Department Memo explaining the hitherto unmentioned event.

In memo below Off. Fouke's denies stopping Zodiac, but provides a highly detailed description of the suspect from what he termed a "five-second drive-by."

[Fouke's partner, Officer Eric Zelms tragically, was killed in the line of duty a month later, but had informed his wife that "Fouke and he had in fact stopped and talked to Zodiac."

The investigating SFPD detective assigned to the Stine murder also confirmed that Fouke acknowledged stopping and talking to Zodiac, but he [detective] decided it was best to let it go and not embarrass the officer or the department.]

Fouke's description:

"Male Caucasian 35 to 45 years ("closer to the high end") 5-10", 180-200, Crew cut hair, pleated baggy pants" was incorporated into the teen's description, results circulated throughout the San Francisco Bay Area.

Additional witness composites were obtained, and all are shown below.

George Hodel 1962   **George Hodel 1974**

SFPD sketch   Joe Barros SFPD sketch   Neal Adams SFPD sketch

Top Row) Photos of GHH in 1962 and 1974. His appearance at the time of Zodiac murders would have to be merged in the viewer's mind. (Age the 1962 photo by seven years or take five years off the 1974 photo.)

(Bottom Row) Shows three separate witness "Zodiac" composites obtained. The "Neal Adams" sketch was drawn by Adams based on combining the two previous witness sketches. The result was used for the cover drawing for a chapter, "This is the Zodiac Speaking" written by journalist Duffy Jennings and

included in a true-crime book, *Great Crimes of San Francisco*, published in 1973.

Neal Adams's composite drawing of the "Zodiac" above an almost a picture-perfect likenss of Dr. George Hill Hodel.

October 19, 1969, *The Tennessean* newspaper article described all of the Bay Area Zodiac crimes and featured the victims.

Surviving gunshot wound victim Michael Mageau included, but no photo was shown. The seventh known Zodiac victim, Cheri Jo Bates (Riverside, California) would not be linked to Zodiac for another year. (November 1970.)

This concludes the limited overview on all twenty-five victims that I consider "Definites" as being murdered by my father, Dr. George Hill Hodel, spanning the years 1943-1969.

These two summary chapters in no way attempt to present all of the evidence in each case. That requires a reading of the complete pentalogy.

The suggested order would be *Black Dahlia Avenger* (Skyhorse/Arcade 2015), *Most Evil* (Dutton 2009), *BDA II* (2014 ed.), *Most Evil II* (Rare Bird Books 2015) and finally the updated *Black Dahlia Avenger III* (Rare Bird Books 2018).

George Hodel was a prolific serial killer whose signature is visable not in any single method of murder, type of victim, or specific killing ground, but rather as a series of complex arrangements, installations and obscure references to art, culture, and film that taken together, reveal a chilling and never-before-documented variety of serial murder: murder as a fine art.

Steve Hodel, *Most Evil*, 2009

POINTS TO PONDER

A trained homicide detective in examining MO and unique crime signatures in *finding three or four that match would have to consider the possibility that a single suspect may have committed and be linked to multiple crimes.*

Here is a list that I believe establishes beyond a reasonable doubt the link between the double homicides of Hazel and Nancy Frome and George Hodel's additional serial crimes committed in the thirty-one years that followed.

Unique crime signatures that he continued to use in Los Angeles, Chicago, Manila, Riverside, and the San Francisco Bay Area.

GEORGE HODEL'S UNIQUE CRIME SIGNATURES

[All of the following crime signatures (19) were used in the Frome's double homicide and used again in varying combinations in George Hodel's (25) subsequent serial crimes from 1943-1969.]

✓ **Serial Killer**

✓ **Meets victims at nightclub and request to dance**

✓ **Handwrites and delivers threat to do harm to victim's person**

✓ **Kidnap Abduction of victims using a vehicle**

✓ **Torture and beating brutal overkill**

✓ **Ligature Strangulation Marks on neck**

- ✓ **Sexual Assault**

- ✓ **Uses cigar or cigarette to burn body**

- ✓ **Undressing and careful posing of victims' bodies postmortem at crime scene**

- ✓ **Severe stomping on victim's nude chest cavity at crime scene**

- ✓ **Dragged bodies short distance in dirt from car**

- ✓ **Used tire iron to inflict blunt force trauma to victim's head and face**

- ✓ **Left man's handkerchief at crime scene**

- ✓ **Likely used medical chloroform to render victim temporarily unconscious during abduction**

- ✓ **Wore gloves left at crime scene**

- ✓ **Lacerates and or removes a piece of flesh from victim's body**

- ✓ **Uses two separate handguns to execute victims**

- ✓ **Leaves behind victims' valuables (watch and diamond rings, robbery not motive)**

- ✓ **"Two men and a woman" involved in the abduction and commission of the murder**

UNIQUE CRIME SIGNATURES OBSERVED PER VICTIM

MM = Mesquite Murders
CL = Chicago District Murders
LW = Lone Woman Murders
ZK = Zodiac

#	Crime Victims →	MM	MM	LW	LW	LW	CL	CL	CL	LW	LW	LW	LW	LW	LW	LW	LW	LW	ZK	ZK	ZK	ZK	ZK	ZK	ZK	ZK	ZK	Indiv. Unique Crime Signatures TOTALS	Percent of Victims with a Specific UCS
		1	2	3	4	5	6	7	8	9	10	11	12	13	14	15	16	17	18	19	20	21	22	23	24	25			
#	**Unique Crime Signatures ↓**	UCS Present	UCS Present	UCS Present	UCS Present	UCS Present	UCS Present	UCS Present	UCS Present	UCS Present	UCS Present	UCS Present	UCS Present	UCS Present	UCS Present	UCS Present	UCS Present	UCS Present	UCS Present	UCS Present	UCS Present	UCS Present	UCS Present	UCS Present	UCS Present	UCS Present		
A	Meets victims at nightclub & requests to dance	✔	✔	✔	✔						✔																5	18.5%
B	Handwrites/delivers threat to do harm to victim's person, family or witness/s	✔	✔		✔		✔	✔	✔	✔	✔		✔	✔	✔	✔			✔		✔	✔	✔	✔	✔	✔	20	74.0%
C	Kidnap Abduction of victims using a vehicle	✔	✔	✔				✔	✔	✔	✔	✔		✔	✔	✔	✔	✔	✔								14	52.0%
D	Ligature Strangulation Marks on neck	✔	✔	✔	✔		✔			✔			✔		✔												9	33.3%
E	Sexual Assault	✔	✔							✔			✔	✔				✔									8	29.6%
F	Uses cigar or cigarette to burn body	✔	✔							✔																	3	11.1%
G	Undressing & careful posing of victim's bodies postmortem at crime scene	✔	✔	✔	✔		✔		✔	✔	✔	✔						✔									10	37.0%
H	Severe stomping on victim's nude chest cavity at crime scene	✔	✔	✔						✔	✔																5	18.5%
I	Dragged bodies short distance in dirt from car	✔	✔							✔																	3	11.1%
J	Used tire iron or similar weapon to inflict blunt force trauma; victim's head & face	✔	✔	✔						✔	✔							✔									6	22.2%
K	Left man's handkerchief at crime scene	✔	✔				✔	✔		✔		✔		✔													6	22.2%
L	Likely used medical ether to render victim temporarily unconscious during	✔	✔				✔	✔	✔	✔		✔		✔													7	25.9%
M	Wore gloves left at crime scene	✔	✔																					✔	✔	✔	5	18.5%
N	Lacerates & or removes a piece of flesh from victim's body	✔	✔				✔	✔	✔	✔			✔	✔				✔	✔					✔	✔		12	44.4%
O	Uses two separate handguns to execute victim	✔	✔																								2	7.4%
P	Leaves behind victim's valuables (watch & diamond rings): robbery not motive	✔	✔	✔	✔	✔	✔	✔	✔	✔	✔							✔	✔	✔	✔	✔	✔	✔	✔	✔	24	88.8%
Q	Two men and a women involved in the abduction and commission of murder	✔	✔					✔	✔	✔			✔														5	18.5%
R	BY KNIFE	✔	✔				✔	✔	✔	✔			✔	✔				✔	✔					✔	✔		13	48.1%
S	BY ROPE	✔	✔	✔	✔				✔	✔		✔	✔		✔				✔					✔	✔		12	44.4%
T	BY GUN	✔	✔					✔												✔	✔	✔	✔	✔	✔	✔	10	37.0%
U	Steals victim's car after a murder and abandons car miles from crime scene	✔	✔		✔									✔													4	14.8%
V	Serial Killer	✔	✔	✔	✔	✔	✔	✔	✔	✔	✔	✔	✔	✔	✔	✔	✔	✔	✔	✔	✔	✔	✔	✔	✔	✔	27	100.0%
#	**Total Number UCS' Per Victim**	22	22	9	8	2	7	6	11	14	11	8	9	4	9	8	3	2	3	6	8	4	4	4	4	8	8	5	
%	**Percentage of UCS's Used Per Victim**	100%	100%	41%	36%	9%	32%	27%	50%	64%	50%	38%	41%	18%	41%	36%	9%	9%	13%	27%	36%	18%	18%	18%	18%	36%	37%	23%	

CODA

<u>Solve:</u> to find a solution, explanation, or answer for

Merriam-Webster Dictionary

In The Mesquite's subtitle reads:

"The Solving of the 1938 West Texas
Kidnap Torture Murders"

Is this case truly solved?

Did my father, **George Hill Hodel** M.D. in the spring of 1938, **along with a male** and **two female accomplices**†, kidnap, torture and sadistically execute Hazel and Nancy Frome and leave their bodies off a remote highway in West Texas?

Have I "found a solution, explanation or answer" that satisfies both sense and reason for this seven decades old whodunit?

Yes, I believe I have.

Have I solved it to a legal certainty "beyond a reasonable doubt" to where a jury would convict Dr. Hodel in a court of law? NO.

Is there enough evidence here presented where the Frome Murders can be "Cleared" by Law Enforcement based on just what has been presented here? NO.

In an earlier chapter, I provided answers that I believe satisfied the three basic requirements for solving this double murder: Method, Opportunity, and Means.

I have also built a case that would easily establish "Probable Cause." That is enough factual evidence that when written and presented as an Affidavit, before a magistrate, it would satisfy the requirements for that judge to issue an arrest and search warrant against Dr. George Hodel both back in 1938 and today.

What is missing?

Let's assume that Dr. George Hodel and Fred Sexton were alive today as were all the original El Paso, Juarez, Mexico and Berkeley, California area witnesses.

Further, let's assume I traded in my Fedora hat and Ford Crown Victoria for a Texas Ranger's Stetson and maybe a good trail horse.

What would I do to attempt to "clear the case"?

My first action would be to execute the court issued search warrant on George Hodel's person, residence and vehicle to see if I could locate the murder weapon(s) and or any connecting evidence such as personal effects belonging to the victims and or any address books or documents linking either Frome name to George Hodel.

Secondly, assuming a live auditorium line-up (my first choice as his voice could be included) was not practical, I would put together a six-photo display card containing my father's 1937 photograph along with five similar appearing males of his approximate age, height, weight and hair coloring.

These would be shown to the various eyewitnesses named in previous chapters. Those viewings may or may not result in a "positive identification" placing George Hodel and or Fred Sexton with the victims during their El Paso/Juarez visit.

Next, I would review all the currently available evidence to see what still remains in custody with El Paso Sheriff's or Texas Rangers Crime Lab, some seven decades later?

These items (rubber gloves, man's handkerchief, patch of short black hair, matchbook cover, wine bottle, bloody tissue papers, newspapers, victims' clothing) could all be processed and vacuumed for "Touch DNA" in an attempt to obtain skin cells for comparison to known DNA of George Hodel currently in my possession.

Finally, I would submit the finalized _Crime Signature and M.O. Chart_ summarizing George Hodel's twenty-five known crimes (1943-1969) in an attempt to include it in the case and filing consideration based on the nineteen similarities between the Frome murders and his later crimes in LA, Chicago, Manila, Riverside, and the San Francisco Bay Area.*

*Note- As a point of criminal law:

"...the prosecution does not have to prove "beyond a reasonable doubt" that the other crimes occurred. Rather, the prosecution simply must present sufficient evidence to show that the act took place and was committed by the defendant."

https://law.jrank.org/pages/8626/Modus-Operandi.html

Depending on the results obtained from the follow-up from both eyewitness identification and or forensic analysis linking George Hodel or Fred Sexton's DNA to the crime; the Frome murder case could likely be "Cleared Other" by El Paso Sheriff's Office or The Texas Rangers.

As a point of information, a homicide case can be "Cleared" whether the *suspect is or is not* actually arrested, prosecuted, and or convicted in a criminal court of law.

The decision to "clear" a homicide remains at the discretion of the investigating agency or department. Usually, it requires the approval of a Commanding Officer.

To further underscore this point and the difference between "Case Solved," and whether or not law enforcement "Clears" a homicide investigation I would refer my readers to the following extensive blog post I presented in June 2019 entitled:

"**Special Report**: Black Dahlia "Voices from the Past": Top City and County Law Enforcement Officers Declare "Case Solved": LAPD Denies Request for DNA Testing, "Too Busy with Current Cases." (Twenty-seven-page photos and text summary)

This "Special Report" post can be found at
www.stevehodel.com/blog

Additional Photographs

Nancy Frome (Circa 1936)

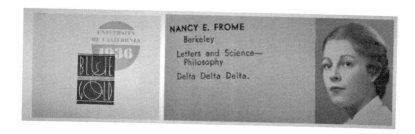

Nancy Frome Berkeley Yearbook 1936

Nancy and mother Hazel seen in earlier trip to
Mexico, July 1937

El Paso Sheriff Chris Fox, (seated) in charge of the nationwide search for the Frome killers seen here with Texas Ranger Captain Red Hawkins.

Berkeley, California
(May 13, 1938)

On left, El Paso County Sheriff Chris Fox, *Director of the Nationwide search for slayers of Hazel & Nancy Frome* confers "on certain new angles" of the double murders with Chief John Greening

Jim Milam, witness saw suspects and victims
together on highway and described suspect
vehicle as "Black Sedan with white lettering on
door panel."

(Milam illiterate was unable to read words.)
Assisted officers in locating bodies in desert.
(April 5, 1938)

Asst. Dist. Attorney William Clayton examines bullets taken from the heads of Hazel and Nancy Frome. "A .32 calibre bullet removed from Mrs. Frome's head and a .38 from Nancy's head indicating to officers that **each woman was slain by a different person.**"

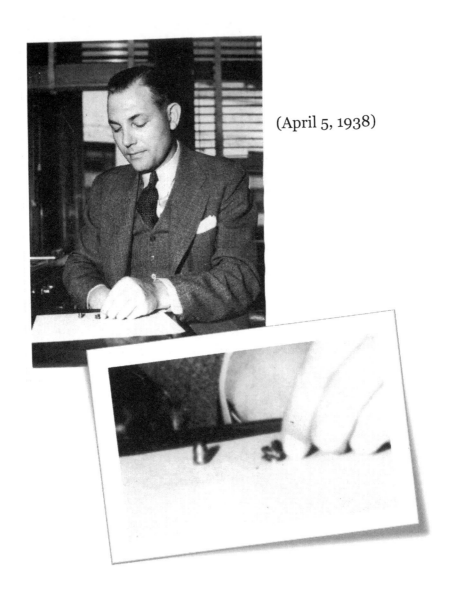

(April 5, 1938)

Rest In Peace

The bodies of Hazel and Nancy Frome were returned to California and the burial services occurred on April 7, *1938, at the Wilson & Keatzer Funeral Chapel* and transferred to the *Sunset View Cemetery,* in Richmond, California for entombment. Grief stricken family follows caskets of Mrs. Frome and daughter, Nancy. Seen above is Weston Frome father and husband supported by his son-in-law and daughter, Lieutenant R.L. McMakin and wife. (4/7/38)

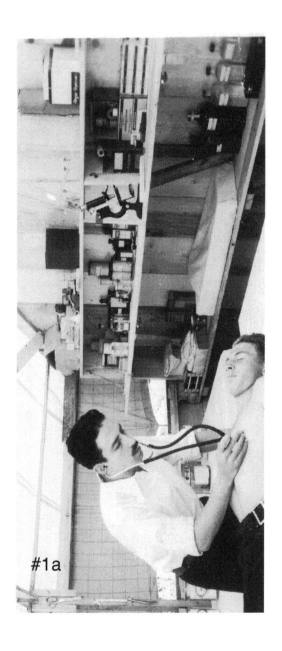

George Hill Hodel M.D. doctoring at clinic in
Santa Fe clinic circa 1937 – Photo #1a

Fred Sexton circa 1945
Possible "Suspect No. 2"in Frome Double Murder

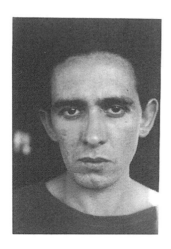 

Below for comparison purposes I have placed the police composite of the Kern killer in between photos of Dr. George Hill Hodel. No mustache was recalled by witnesses, thus I have intentionally 'airbrushed' it out to show how Hodel would have appeared in the late 1940s and early 50s.

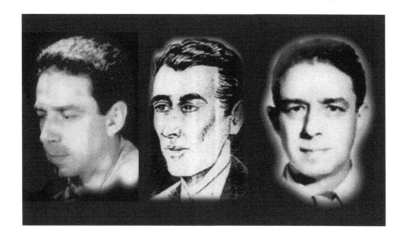

May 2, 1938
Dr. Romano Nicholas Trotsky (Photo above left) and a second unnamed
doctor were arrested & questioned by police in Frome killings

"...Investigators into the slaying of Mrs. Weston G.
Frome and her daughter, Nancy, today questioned
two physicians, one at Lufkin, Tex., and one at San
Angelo, as possible suspects.

*...Finding of a pair of **rubber gloves, wrapped** in a **San Francisco newspaper**, along with other articles that may have been part of the Frome baggage, near Balmorhea, made **probable** the **theory** that the **murders** were **committed** by a **person with "medical knowledge."***

The fact that both suspects stayed at the hotel where the Frome women lived also fitted with Sheriff Fox's theory that the two Berkeleyites were slain by an acquaintance—possibly made in El Paso.

...Dr. Trotsky was arrested Saturday at San Angelo. He was known to have stayed at the Cortez hotel in El Paso where the Frome Women lived during their five-day stay here."

Nota bene:

Both doctors were subsequently **released** and **cleared** from suspicion, but investigators continued to **believe** that the **actual suspect(s)** may have been **a doctor** or **someone** with **medical training**.

This information also tends to confirm, as reported earlier, "that a medical convention was believed ongoing at the Cortez Hotel during the week of the Fromes arrival at the hotel."

†Second Female Accomplice Linked to Frome Murders

(re † see CODA page 181)

"**Witnesses** also told of **seeing two women**, apparently neither Mrs. Frome nor her daughter, **driving the Frome automobile the day of the murders**. ...described them as a blonde of about 24 and a brunette of about 30."

New York Daily News
April 6, 1938

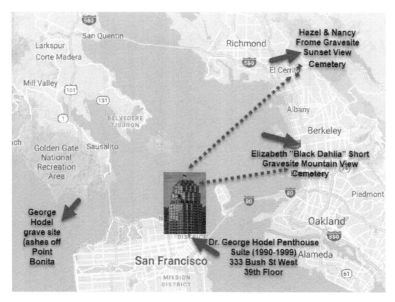

This diagram shows the proximity of the Frome and Short grave sites in the Oakland/El Cerrito East Bay Area. From 1990 until his death in 1999, Dr. George Hill Hodel resided in a 39th floor condominium in downtown San Francisco. (333 Bush Street West) Both the Sunset View Cemetery (Fromes) and the Mountain View Cemetery (Elizabeth "Black Dahlia" Short) could be seen using a telescope from his residence. George Hodel's ashes (location shown above) were cast to sea directly off Point Bonita just beyond the Golden Gate Bridge.

Dr. George Hill Hodel circa 1998 a year before his death seen looking out his floor to ceiling bay view window from the 39th Floor of his residence. He frequently used a large telescope that was permanently set up in his living room. From his vantage point he was able to view both the Oakland Bay and the Golden Gate bridges and across to the East Bay which included both the Frome/Short burial sites.

Author's photograph of June (left) & George Hodel (right) circa 1997 view from their 39th floor penthouse suite of San Francisco Bay. *Arrow in circle* marks one leg of a tripod supporting a large telescope the remainder of which is blocked from view by June's body.

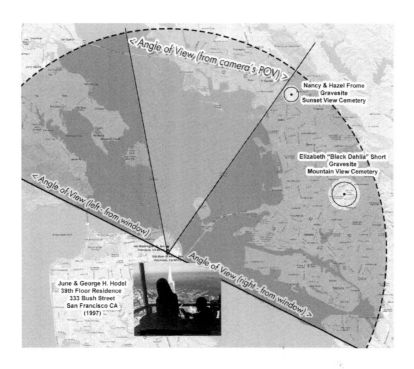

This diagram shows the 'camera's eye' view (the center wedge) with June and George Hodel between the Author/Camera and the window. Standing at the window the arc shows the 180 degree view available.

This view encompasses the final resting places of Nancy & Hazel Frome (dot in small circle above - Sunset View Cemetery) and Elizabeth Short's gravesite (dot in larger circle below – Mountain View Cemetery).

**Enlargement of Boomhower purse
(from page 135 & 137)**

handwritten note:

POLICE DEPT.—
WE FOUND THIS
AT BEACH
THURSDAY NIGHT

Addendum to
GEORGETTE BAUERDORF— on pages 86-87
"The Bathtub Murder" (MURDER WEAPON)

October 11, 1944, Los Angeles
(Los Angeles Sheriff's Department)

Evidence Shows Heiress Waged Terrific Fight

Bruises and Fist Marks Found on Her Body;
Light Over Door Found Twisted to Darken Place

FOUGHT FOR LIFE — Autopsy examinations showed
Georgette Bauerdorf put up terrific battle for life against
man who attacked her in apartment at 8400 Fountain Ave.

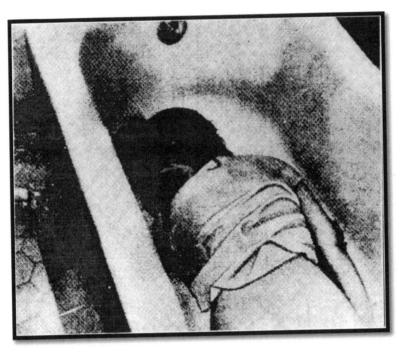

Photo of victim Bauerdorf in her apartment tub. Killer placed body in tub after death as no water was found in lungs at autopsy. Cause of death was asphyxiation using a **9" medical bandage** taken from a larger roll: **the murder weapon**.

Photo of the 9"-wide medical bandage used to aspyxiate Georgette Bauerdorf on Oct. 12, 1944.

Detectives ascertained this large size elastic type bandage was quite rare and had not been sold in the Los Angeles area for over 22 years.

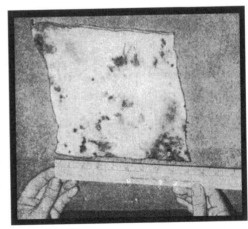

RARE ELASTIC CLOTH STRANGLED HEIRESS

Hollywood, Oct. 19 (UP)—The cloth that strangled Oil Heiress Georgette Bauerdorf came from a rare, imported elastic bandage material that has not been sold locally for more than 20 years, sheriff's investigators discovered today.

Deputies, who had previously worked under the belief the cloth was a piece of toweling, found a two-inch-wide matching piece of material, called crepe tetra, at a medical supply establishment. They said the large size had not been sold here for 22 years.

The rubberless material is made with a peculiar weave that gives it elasticity.

"We can now begin the hunt for whoever was wearing such a bandage," Inspector Penprase said.

An inquest will be held tomorrow into the death of the attractive Hollywood canteen hostess, whose half clad body was found last Thursday face down in the bathtub of her luxurious apartment.

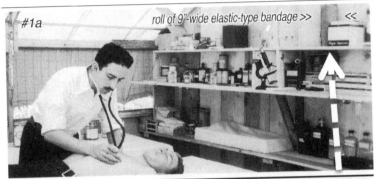

#1a — roll of 9"-wide elastic-type bandage >> <<

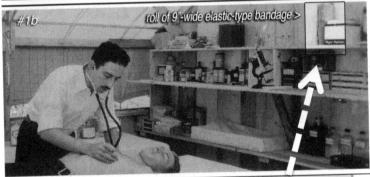

#1b — roll of 9"-wide elastic-type bandage >

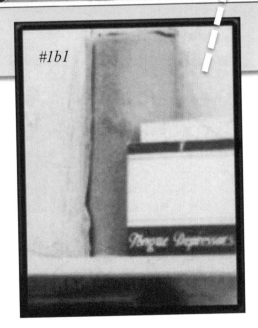

#1b1

Care, Custody, & Control

Dr. George Hodel seen in (*Photo #1a* on the previous page) doctoring to patient in his Santa Fe, NM clinic in 1937-1938.

Photo #1b [a higher contrast image of *#1a*] shows a roll of 9" roll of elastic-type bandage standing on the top shelf (highlighted upper right hand corner) of 'medical stores' or supplies under the care, custody and control of Dr. George Hill Hodel.

The enlarged *inset photo #1b1* (from *#1b*) shows a 9" roll of elastic-type bandage* identical in description to that used to asphyxiate Bauerdorf—e.g., GHH had care, custody, & control in 1937-8 the same type item.

Nota bene: Based on GHH's known M.O. it is possible that upon accosting victim inside her apt he used the bandage (likely to have been carried in his doctor's "black bag"), and soaked it in chloroform to subdue , then rape her and force the bandage down her throat. Cause of death found to be asphyxiation from this medical bandage. Victim then transported to the tub which was filled with water prior to suspect leaving apartment. In 1945 LA Sheriff's detectives would investigate a possible connection of this Bauerdorf "Bathtub Murder" to two unsolved Chicago "Bathtub Murders" which later became known as the "Chicago Lipstick Murders." *As previously indicated those crimes were also committed by Dr. George Hill Hodel.*

(*elastic-type bandage commonly referred to today by the "Ace" brand name as 'an ace bandage'.)

Approximate Location of 1938 Frome Murder Scene

As It Looks Today
April 2019

Personal Note to
El Paso Sheriff's Office
and
Texas DPS, Criminal Division, Austin Texas

I want to direct a closing thought to my fellow officers currently assigned to Cold Case Investigations at either the El Paso Sheriff's Office or the Texas Department of Public Safety, Criminal Division in Austin.

I would respectfully suggest that one of your active investigators pick up the telephone and check with your Austin Crime Lab to see if any of the many evidentiary items previously described as being recovered from the Frome crime scene and booked in evidence, still exist?

Perhaps in a Property Section or warehouse? We know that some items were retained by El Paso Sheriffs and others sent to the Austin Crime Lab for analysis.

If testing proves positive for "stranger DNA" I will gladly provide El Paso Sheriffs or Texas DPS my father's full DNA profile, currently in my possession, for comparison.

Most Sincerely,

Steve Hodel
Los Angeles, California
Email: steve@stevehodel.com

Acknowledgements

First and foremost, I would like to acknowledge Mr. Ron Dawson, who in 2014, first emailed me his suspicions that "there might be a link between your father, Dr. George Hill Hodel and the long forgotten West Texas 1938 Double homicide of Hazel and Nancy Frome." Had Ron not contacted me and suggested I "take a look," there likely would have been no investigation and no book.

Secondly, my sincere gratitude and appreciation to my good friend former Dallas Police officer, author of 14 novels and one true-crime book, 7 volumes of poetry and a photographer extraordinaire, Robert J. Sadler. (robertjsadler.com/author/)

Robert has been my friend for many years and my "partner" and true "sidekick" throughout the Frome investigation and along that dusty trail, has provided me with much wise counsel and objectivity. Robert has assisted in the editing and formatting of this book, as well as conducting some photography at the original Frome crime scene location, near Van Horn, Texas, as seen in earlier chapters of this book. Additionally, Robert designed and created the covers for *In The Mesquite*. Mucho Gracias Amigo.

A five paws way up "thank you" and big bear hug to my good buddy and fellow Angeleno, Hermann H. who, with his pooka-like presence, has once again come to my aid and assistance in sharing his profound thoughts and insights.

Thanks to Dr. Doug Lyle for his always pitch perfect analysis and advice on questions of medical forensics.

The book title credit *"In The Mesquite"* goes to Alaskan screenwriter/playwright, Dave Hunsaker, a good friend and confidant from the start of this investigation who to my mind gave us the perfect title.

Finally, let me thank all of my readers both here in the U.S. and abroad for expressing your continued support and confidence in my ongoing investigations. Your thousands of "comments" and shared "clues" at both my author blog site (www.stevehodel.com/blog) and Facebook page are a great encouragement.

Wishing All My Very Best,

Steve Hodel
Los Angeles, California
July 8, 2019

Former Dallas Officer / PI & former LAPD Det. III / PI
The friends & authors have lunch at Musso & Frank

Friends finally meet, share cops & writers stories.

ABOUT THE AUTHOR

Steve Hodel is a *New York Times bestselling author. He spent twenty-four years with the LAPD, where, as a homicide detective, he worked on more than three hundred murder cases and achieved one of the highest "solve rates" on the force. He is a licensed PI and author and his first book,* Black Dahlia Avenger: A Genius for Murder *was a New York Times bestseller and was nominated for an MWA Edgar Award in the Best Fact category. Steve has written four additional books:* Most Evil, *a Los Angeles Times bestseller,* Black Dahlia Avenger II, *a sequel and an eight-year follow-up to his true-crime investigations and the recently published* Most Evil II *(Rare Bird Books, 2015). A* fifth book, Black Dahlia Avenger III: *Murder as a Fine Art,* published in November 2018. *His investigations, spanning two decades have been featured on NBC Dateline, CBS 48 Hours, Court TV, A&E Bill Kurtis, Cold Case Files, CNN Anderson Cooper, and the Discovery Channel. Steve most recently appeared in March 2019 on the* Today Show and Dr. Phil *and Dr. Oz, where he with other family members discussed the making of the No. 1 national hit podcast,* Root of Evil: The True Story of the Hodel Family and the Black Dahlia Murder. *Steve resides in his hometown of Los Angeles.*

~

PRAISE FOR STEVE'S PREVIOUS BOOKS

"Crime was rampant as musicals in Los Angeles in the postwar years—this is the age of Bugsy Siegel, the founding of Las Vegas, Mickey Cohen and gun battles on Sunset Boulevard....and it's the age of film noir....George Hodel, I think is fit company for some of noir's most civilized villains—like Waldo Lydecker in *Laura*, Harry Lime in *The Third Man*, or even Noah Cross in *Chinatown*."

—**DAVID THOMSON**, *New York Times Book Review*

"The most haunting murder mystery in Los Angeles County during the twentieth century has finally been solved."

—**STEPHEN R. KAY**, L.A. County Head Deputy District Attorney

"Los Angeles is the construct of its mythologies good and bad, fact, and fiction. The legend of Elizabeth Short is one of the most enduring. Hodel's investigation is thoroughly and completely convincing. So too is this book. As far as I am concerned, this case is closed."

—**MICHAEL CONNELLY**, *New York Times* bestselling author of the Harry Bosch novels and television series.

"From this distance, there is no doubt that George Hodel committed/performed theatrical murders in several cities over several decades. That a mad doctor's son grew up to be a detective and solved a master criminal's surrealist crimes—and it was his father—is mind-blowing. But, there it is. My deepest and sincerest respect for [Steve's] fearless and brilliant investigation into a profound darkness that [he has] brought into a penetrating light."

--**T-BONE BURNETT**, Oscar, Grammy, and Golden Globe Award-winning musician, songwriter, Music Director, "True Detective."

"A whodunit masterpiece that solves one of the most infamous series of murders of the last century. Shockingly, but sans a shadow of a doubt, former Hollywood homicide detective Steve Hodel fingers a man he well knew: his own father. For fans of true crime and police procedurals, *Most Evil II* is a must read."

BRUCE HENDERSON, NYT Bestselling author of *And the Sea Will Tell* and *Sons and Soldiers*.

"Steve Hodel's hunt for the Black Dahlia murderer and the Zodiac killer is the grand cinemascope version of every unsolved serial murder case. Now, in his new nonfiction thriller, he delves into codes and ciphers, the world of the kinky avant-garde, and new and shocking secrets about the investigation of the Zodiac killer. Most Evil II is as compelling as his other books and adds to the body of work that is, without a doubt, both the strangest and the most compelling investigation of our day."

--**GERALD PETIEVICH**, author of *The Sentinel* and *To Live and Die in L.A.*

"A must-read book . . . A blockbuster."

—**LIZ SMITH**, *New York Post*

"Fascinating."

—**JOHNNY DEPP**

"An ex-L.A. cop uncovers a painful answer to the notorious 1947 Black Dahlia slaying...Hodel appears to have solved one of the most sensational murders in the history of Los Angeles."

—*PEOPLE MAGAZINE*

"In this 2003 case study, Hodel declares the case is solved. He offers irrefutable evidence piled fact upon fact as only the mind of a professional detective can present. *The Black Dahlia Avenger* is packaged as neatly as a court deposition."

—ST. AUGUSTINE RECORD

"[Hodel] has written an intensely readable account....So what's the final verdict on *Black Dahlia Avenger*? Its accounts of cover-ups and civic corruption are all too believable, and much of the circumstantial evidence it presents against George Hodel is persuasive.... Has Steve Hodel solved the case? I think so."

—JON L. BREEN, *The Weekly Standard*

"An absorbing, thought-provoking and insightful read from beginning to end, *Black Dahlia Avenger III* is an extraordinary study and one that will be an enduringly popular addition to community and academic library Criminology collections, as well as the personal reading lists of all True Crime buffs."

—MIDWEST BOOK REVIEW

"[Steve Hodel] gives us a fascinating family psychodrama; we watch his image of his father morph from flawed but lovable ladies' man to monster."

—NEWSWEEK

"The book has been described as 'Hannibal Lecter meets *L.A. Confidential* meets *Chinatown*,' but even that Hollywood characterization doesn't do it justice. Former Los Angeles police detective Steve Hodel has written one of the most compelling true-crime books of all time."

—SEATTLE WEEKLY

"[Hodel] makes a strong case that the Black Dahlia was part of a larger series of ritual murders that went on for years. This unsparing, chilling account of the actions of a perfect psychopath grips to the end."

—TORONTO GLOBE AND MAIL

"Hodel tells the story well and with incredible objectivity. . . . A real-life tale of Dr. Jekyll and Mr. Hyde."

—RICHMOND TIMES-DISPATCH

"This remarkable book will keep readers riveted from the first page to the very last."

—CITIZEN

"*Black Dahlia Avenger* is a fascinating and horrifying tale of 1940s Los Angeles-as Steve Hodel says, a real-life *L.A. Confidential.*"

—SAN JOSE MERCURY-NEWS

"The story boasts all the glamour and sinister mystique of film noir."

—THE DAILY TELEGRAPH

"Readers must hang on tightly as Hodel hurtles along on his compelling parallel journeys of discovery—a return to the melodramatic days of old Hollywood and a simultaneous plunge into the dark roots of his own family tree.

—LONDON FREE PRESS

PRAISE FOR *In The Mesquite*

"Steve Hodel delivers again with this masterful and gripping chapter of his two-decade investigation into the most prolific killer the world had never known—his father, Dr. George Hill Hodel. With *In The Mesquite*, Steve Hodel has again built a compelling and skillful investigation that leads to only one logical suspect for the 1938 brutal murders of Hazel and Nancy Frome: his father. In this riveting one-off chapter of the murderous career of George Hodel, Steve Hodel leaves his reader begging for more."

—*ALISA STATMAN* Director and Bestselling author of *RESTLESS SOULS: The Sharon Tate Family's Account of Stardom, the Manson Murders, and a Crusade for Justice*

~

"Steve Hodel has done it again! Following the leads, the evidence and the circumstances surrounding the murders of Hazel and Nancy Frome, Steve has put his nose to the grindstone and solved this grisly crime, committed by his father, Dr. George Hill Hodel. Read the later chapters for undeniable links between this 1938 tragedy and so many others committed in the years to come by the same man. The evidence speaks for itself and has been brought to bear by one of the nation's most seasoned and dogged detectives. Bravo, Steve! "

—*KAREN SMITH*, M.S. Retired Major Case Detective, Jacksonville Sheriff's Office, Forensic Expert for CNN, HLN, Nancy Grace

~

As a collaborator with Steve in getting his book *In The Mesquite* into print, I am biased. However that does not preclude me from offering my opinion.

My observation of Steve Hodel's life's work, his investigations, his books is that he laboriously and meticulously gathers information and corroborates all the facts that can be corroborated. To those facts he brings to bear over fifty years of investigative know-how and experience to support every aspect of his suppositions and conclusions. His unquestioned integrity remains the cornerstone of his investigative ethos: discover the facts, analyze the facts, let the facts connect where they will and report those facts.

As with Steve's other books *In the Mesquite* is presented not to convince you he is right, but to provide you with logical proofs and inferences as to who did what, when, where, and how. It is up to the reader to agree or disagree. Steve says, as noted on the cover, this book is about "SOLVING" the case, not saying 'IT IS CLEARED". Without physical evidence to forensically test (such as DNA testing) or the ability to interview long-gone fact witnesses, the case will likely never be "cleared" or adjudicated in a court of law.

If you disagree with Steve's solutions, that is your prerogative. But what is the purpose of disagreeing if you cannot supply a more well thought through, logical or proven solution—particularly when you consider the nineteen unique crime signatures identified *In The Mesquite* that also appear in other murders attributed to Doctor George Hill Hodel.

—*ROBERT J. SADLER*, former Dallas Police Officer, Crime Analyst, Private Investigator, Security Consultant and author of: the true-crime book - *One Step from Murder, the Friendly Burglar Rapist,* and fourteen novels.

~

ALSO, BY STEVE HODEL

~

Black Dahlia Avenger
(Arcade/Skyhorse 2015)

Most Evil
(Dutton 2009)

Black Dahlia Avenger II
(Thoughtprint Press 2014)

Most Evil II
(Rare Bird Books 2015)

Black Dahlia Avenger III
(Rare Bird Books 2018)

Recommended Reading Order by Numbers

Visit the author's blog site:

(www.stevehodel.com/blog)

Printed in Poland
by Amazon Fulfillment
Poland Sp. z o.o., Wrocław

48367974R00129